G000255709

EPSOM

EPSOM

Its History & Its Surroundings

by
GORDON HOME

With a new Foreword
by
JOHN DENT

Republished S.R. Publishers, Ltd., 1971
First published Epsom and London, 1901

Bibliographic Note

The reader will appreciate that the Golf Club and Rifle Club fees and subscriptions given on pages 186 and 187 were those applicable in 1901.

Republished 1971 by S.R. Publishers Limited,
East Ardsley, Wakefield,
Yorkshire, England
by kind permission of the
copyright holders

Reprinted 1972

© New Introduction S.R. Publishers Limited

ISBN 0 85409 736 8

Please address all enquiries to S.R. Publishers Ltd.
(address as above)

Reprinted by Scolar Press Ltd.,
Menston, Yorkshire, U.K.

FOREWORD

Although seventy years have elapsed since this book was first published, it remains the latest and best description and history of the town which Gordon Home knew so well. It was the second book to come from the pen of an author who was to achieve fame as a writer and illustrator of topographical and historical books.

Born in 1878, he served in the 1914-18 War as a Major in the R.A.S.C. He travelled extensively, particularly in North Africa and through many parts of the British Empire. In recent years he lived at Waverley Abbey House, Farnham, moving to Fittleworth, near Pulborough, shortly before his death on 13th December, 1969.

Before he was 23, he wrote and illustrated this book, and the work was so well done that it still has a freshness and a readability not found in the heavy, copiously footnoted writings of latter-day historians of other towns.

Inevitably, in seventy years, some of the buildings he described or drew have disappeared or been modified almost beyond recognition. These losses have not all been as serious as the tragedy of Pitt Place, with its historical associations with Nonsuch Palace. At the other end of the spectrum, not even the most ardent protectionist could regret the quite recent passing of "Rabbit Hutch Row", the tiny timber cottages with shop fronts in the High Street. The narrow eastern end of the High Street which Gordon Home knew was widened in 1938, although the building of the shops was not completed until after the war. The Public Hall was demolished in 1934, and the site is now the Quadrant. Commuters no longer pour out of the station in Upper High Street, or Station Road, as it was in 1901. East Street, formerly a bedraggled and unprepossessing approach to the town from the north, is well on the way to achieving a dignity in keeping with the rest of Epsom. The Race Week residents on the Downs no longer troop down Church Street to wash in the horse-trough at that end of the High Street. Twenty years ago the famous Well water was pronounced unfit for human consumption. In many other ways the Epsom of to-day and the Epsom of 1901 are poles apart.

How refreshing, then, to see that so much of our heritage remains. Everywhere in the book there are familiar landmarks: a tribute to the efforts of those who, particularly in recent years, have striven hard to prevent Epsom degenerating into just another suburban wasteland.

At this critical period in the life of the town, the re-issue of this book is a timely reminder that the Epsom of to-day has roots going deep into the past, and that the Epsom of tomorrow will be the poorer if many more of these roots are severed.

JOHN DENT

DURDANS.

The Epsom Seat of the Right Hon. The Earl of Rosebery, K.G.

EPSOM

Its History & its Surroundings
By Gordon Home
Illustrated by
The Author.

WITH AN INTRODUCTION.

THE HOMELAND ASSOCIATION, LD.,

EPSOM : L. W. Andrews & Son, High Street.
LONDON : St. Bride's House, 24 Bride Lane, Fleet Street.

1901.

CONTENTS.

		PAGE
Preface	. . . .	*7*
List of Illustrations	. . . .	*8*
Bibliography	. . . .	*10*
Introduction	. . . .	*11*

Chapter   *I.—The position of Epsom, and a general description of the Town and District* . . . *21*

,,   *II.—Concerning Epsom from the earliest times to the present day* *25*

,,   *III.—In which an attempt is made to describe Epsom in the 17th century* *43*

,.   *IV.—In which an Account is given of the Churches of Epsom* *64*

,,   *V.—A description of Woodcote, Durdans, and some other great Houses* *78*

,,   *VI.—Concerning some Worthies of Epsom* . . *101*

,,   *VII.—How the Downs became famous for Horse-Racing* *108*

,,   *VIII.—In which the Country beyond the Downs is described* *116*

,,   *IX.—A description of the Country West of the Town* *135*

,,   *X.—A description of the Country North of the Town* *145*

,,   *XI.—On the Birds of Epsom and the District* . *179*

,,   *XII.—Golf at Epsom* *184*

,,   *XIII.—Road Distances* *188*

INDEX *191*

Map of the District

PREFACE.

In the compilation of this little book I have received much help from a large number of residents in and around Epsom. My thanks are especially due to Lord Rosebery, the Rev. E. W. Northey, Mr. A. W. Aston, Dr. W. Clement Daniel, the Rev. C. H. Rice of Cheam and the Rev. P. Mordaunt Barnard, of Headley, also to Mr. Dearle and Mr. Charles Young who placed their long memories as residents in Epsom at my disposal.

To Mr. John A. Bucknill and to Mr. G. F. Burgess I tender my thanks for the special chapters they have contributed.

GORDON HOME.

CROMWELL LODGE,
    EPSOM,
        June 30, 1901.

LIST OF ILLUSTRATIONS.

PAGE

Durdans, the Epsom Seat of the Right Honourable the Earl
    of Rosebery, K.G. . . . . . . *Frontispiece*

The "New Inn" (now known as "Waterloo House") in High
    Street, Epsom   23

High Street, Epsom, showing the old Watch House . .   30

High Street, Epsom, with the Clock Tower . . .   33

"Spread Eagle" Hotel   35

Sketch and Plan of the upper floor of the "New Inn" . .   46

A portion of the staircase in the "New Inn" . .   47

Nell Gwynne, from the painting by Sir Peter Lely .   49

A birds-eye view of Epsom as it appeared about 1700 .   56

Trees in the Dorking Road   61

The Well as it appears to-day   63

Epsom Parish Church   65

Carved Mahogany Chest in Epsom Church . . .   67

Christ Church, Epsom Common   72

Sir Edward Northey   79

Frederick Prince of Wales   85

Mr. Arthur Heathcote   87

The "Amato Inn" at Woodcote   90

Firegrate at Woodcote Grove   91

Woodcote Grove   92

Lord Lyttelton's Bedroom in Pit Place . . .   96

Carved Stone Figure in Pit Place   98

The Prince of Wales, afterwards George IV . . . 102

Mrs. Mapp, the Bone-setter 105

Coursing on Epsom Downs 110

The Grand Stand 113

Headley Heath 121

Leaden Font in Walton-on-the-Hill Church . . . 123

On Walton Heath 125

Chipstead Church 128

The Well House at Banstead 130

Banstead Church from the West 132

The Dorking Road 137

At Oxshott 138

Ashtead Church 141

Ewell, High Street 146

The Watch House in Church Street, Ewell . . 147

The Tower and Graveyard of Ewell Old Church . . 149

Foundations of the Banqueting Hall of Nonsuch Palace . 155

Nonsuch Palace, from an old engraving . . . 161

Lady Castlemaine, Duchess of Cleveland, after Sir Peter Lely 165

White Hall, Cheam 168

Brass, representing the Trinity, in the Lumley Chapel at Cheam 170

Fanny Burney (Madame D'Arblay) 176

BIBLIOGRAPHY.

Manning and Bray's History of Surrey.

Brayley's History of Surrey.

The Diary of Samuel Pepys, F.R.S.

The Diary of John Evelyn, F.R.S.

Diary and Letters of Madame D'Arblay.

John Aubrey's Natural History and Antiquities of Surrey. 1719.

Antiquities of Surrey. By N. Salmon. 1736.

A Collection of several pieces of Mr. John Toland. 1726.

Schoberl's Beauties and Antiquities.

History of Epsom. H. Pownall. 1825.

Swete's Handbook of Epsom. 1851.

Men I have known. By Wm. Jerdan. 1866.

Lyson's Environs of London.

Greater London. Edward Walford, M.A.

Camden's Britannia.

Domestic State Papers.

The Registers of Banstead in the County of Surrey. 1896.

Fuller's Worthies of Surrey.

Gentleman's Magazine. Vols. 57 and 83.

The Battle of Epsom : a new Ballad. 1763.

Memoirs of Mrs. Fitzherbert. By The Hon. Charles Langdale. 1856.

Canon Isaac Taylor's Words and Places. 1865.

Canon Isaac Taylor's Names and their Histories. 1896.

Larwood & Hotten's History of Signboards.

Passages from the Diary of Mrs. Phillip Lybbe Powys. Edited by Emily J. Climenson.

The Letters of Horace Walpole.

INTRODUCTION.

I AM desired to write a few words of preface to a Handbook for Epsom. And, when one comes to think of it, one must write it soon, for there will soon be little material for a preface or a guide.

When I first came to live at Epsom, a quarter of a century ago, it was a little sleepy town, surrounded by long stretches of down and common. Its perennial slumber was broken twice a year by race meetings, when the followers and camp followers of the Turf stormed the neighbourhood during a few agitated days, then struck their tents and left the town, sodden and exhausted. Thereafter the calm recommenced, and the inhabitants could saunter over miles of open turf to breathe the purest air in England. But the memory of those six days of carnival kept off the speculative builder and his serious clients. Thus the town remained rural and old fashioned. Now all that is changed. The clients of the builder have reconsidered their objections, and so he has come and cut into the lanes and hedges. A gaunt asylum shrouds the misery of hundreds or thousands of the mad patients of London. One or two commons are enclosed. The stray edges of greenery, which were the heritage of the wayfarer, are being gradually fenced in. A new railroad, traversing a rural desert, lands its stray passengers on to a belated bull-ring, which tops the downs with its aggressive bulk. It is all, I suppose, necessary, nay inevitable. But these changes have killed the old Epsom. The new Epsom is only a fragment of the past, and only a fragment of the future.

Long ago, Epsom was fashionable. Charles the Second raced here and played bowls here. Prince George of Denmark, the husband of Queen Anne, came here and drank the waters. Frederick Prince of Wales lived here, enjoyed hawking on the Downs, and it is said fought a chimney-sweep, sustaining defeat. But the glorious epoch of Epsom seems to have ended with the seventeenth century. The stay of Frederick Prince of Wales at Epsom was in its unfashionable days; perhaps he only came to court obscurity when in conflict with his father. It is difficult indeed to ascertain when he was at Epsom, in spite of the strong local tradition and the statement of Horace Walpole that he actually owned Durdans. Probably he went on a visit to Lord Guilford, who did own Durdans, and who was a Lord of his Bedchamber. But in any case the chalybeate or cathartic glories of Epsom had then passed away.

When and whence were those glories? It appears that in the later years of Queen Elizabeth the waters had been obscurely, indeed parochially, drunk; and in the middle of the seventeenth century foreigners were said to come from abroad for that purpose. It was, however, the demolition of the neighbouring Palace of Nonsuch which launched Epsom on its brief career as a watering place; for the great structure furnished much building material, and so was a quarry out of which were erected dwellings in a sumptuous style, new to the country village. This was in 1670, for in that year Charles II had given Nonsuch to Barbara Villiers, who lost no time in converting it into cash.

Our local historian, Mr. Pownall, who published his little book in 1825, lingers fondly over those glorious times. "Soon after the improvements made by Mr. Parkhurst at the Wells (about 1690), the village was enlarged to a considerable extent. It became the centre of fashion; several houses were erected for lodgings, and yet the place would not contain all the visitors, many of whom were obliged to seek for accommodation in the neighbouring villages. Taverns, at that time reputed to be the largest in England, were opened; sedan chairs and numbered coaches attended. There was a public breakfast, with dancing and music, every morning at the wells. There was also a ring, as in Hyde Park; and on the downs, races were held daily at noon; with cudgelling and wrestling matches, foot races, &c., in the afternoon. The evenings were usually spent in private parties, assemblies, or cards; and we may add, that neither Bath nor Tunbridge ever boasted of more noble visitors than Epsom, or exceeded it in splendour, at the time we are describing."

In spite of this glowing description, I am inclined to doubt whether Epsom was ever fashionable in the sense in which that epithet is applied to Tunbridge Wells or Bath. It was probably the haunt rather of the middle classes than of noble visitors. That at least is the impression left by Shadwell's coarse comedy. It may be noted, too, that a great number of letters from great people were dated from Bath, but few or none from Epsom. The houses of Bath, too, are redolent with the tradition of sublime names. There are scarcely any such at Epsom. Lord Berkeley, no doubt, had his house and entertained his friends. We have a glimpse of Lord Buckhurst and Sir Charles Sedley flirting with Nell Gwynne in the High Street. Lord Baltimore led a

debauched life at Woodcote.   Lord Lyttelton closed a
debauched life at Pit Place.   But these noble names
almost exhaust the record.   And the visitors to the
town who believed in the virtue of the waters, while
they were cured at least as much by air, abstinence,
exercise, and a healing faith, as by the merits of the well,
were, it may be surmised, in the main what were called
"cits."   This does not imply that they were not as gay
and as profitable as the gouty statesmen and nobles who
sought health and gambling tables elsewhere.

In spite of Prince George of Denmark the decline of
Epsom began, we are told by our historian, in 1704.
The "knavery of an apothecary" was, it appears,
sufficient to put an end to our career of brilliancy.   This
miscreant bought land, sunk a well, erected ball rooms,
gambling rooms and a pump.   Shops too "for milliners,
jewellers and toymen," and a bowling green were there.
His advertisements were indeed alluring.   There was a
"variety of raffling-shops, attended every day by a fine
consort of musick;" there were cockfights and horse-
races ; there were also empty shops for "a bookseller,
pictures, a haberdasher of hats, shoomaker, fishmonger
and butcher, with conveniences for several other trades."
The centre of these attractions he called the New Wells.
Where this guilty paradise was situated I do not know;
but as a source of health it was deceptive.   "The water
of the New Wells did not possess any virtue, and
consequently those who drank it did not derive any
benefit therefrom."   So sighs Pownall, but as nothing
was charged for the waters, it may perhaps be said that
their want of quality constituted no direct fraud on the
public.   Worse than all, the old and virtuous wells, full

of healing, "grew into unmerited disrepute, for want of a distinction." Still in all this, though there may have been folly and presumption, there was no actual iniquity. The crime of the man of medicine remains to be told. He procured a lease of the Old Wells and locked them up till he died (in 1727). Are there any waters in the world which could triumph over treatment of this kind?

Toland, who wrote in 1711, under the hollow and glittering reign of the wicked apothecary, penned a glowing description, which will be found in this book. And yet, though the scene that he describes is brilliant and animated, within four years of this period, Epsom was, according to Pownall, gradually deserted owing to the "knavish tricks" of the spurious healer.

In 1720 there was another brief swell of prosperity, not of the surest, when the South Sea Bubble for a time filled Epsom with its train of speculators and adventurers: "alchemists, Dutchmen, Germans, Jews;" and "gaming with every other description of profligacy and vice, prevailed to an enormous extent." And at that period several large houses were erected, "amongst them that of Baron Swasso."

Who Baron Swasso may have been we cannot guess— though his name rings like that of a possible alchemist— but at any rate he did not arrest the decadence of Epsom. The South Sea Bubble burst and Epsom fell once more. In 1736 the celebrated "Female Bone-Setter," a Mrs. Mapp, gave us a temporary glamour of popularity, though it was but a flicker. The "neighbouring gentry however continued their patronage, and every Monday in the summer they came to the Wells and had a public breakfast with music, dancing, and cards till about three o'clock." There is a pathetic advertisement in 1754, quite in the modern indirect style, which aims at stimulating this fleeting fashion.

"EPSOM OLD WELL. The Gentlemen and Ladies who did me the honour to breakfast at this place last Monday morning have signified their pleasure of breakfasting here every Monday during the Season; I take this opportunity to return my unfeigned thanks for the favour of so genteel an appearance, and humbly hope for the continuance of the same, which will lay under the greatest obligation their most humble servant JANE HAWKINS. Note. The Purging Waters of this place are in excellent order."

But even this genteel appearance and the attractions mentioned in the Note failed to stimulate the flagging repute of the faded watering place, and Epsom "became (as it now remains) a populous, wealthy and respectable village, without retaining any of its former dissipated and vicious sources of amusing."

The vogue of Bath and of sea-bathing gave Epsom the final death-stroke, as a health resort; "the modern delightful practice of sea-bathing," as Pownall forgivingly calls it. When people began to bathe in the sea, they seem indeed to have become demoralised. "The well is preserved . . . but is now only visited occasionally by strangers who, not having faith in the mineral waters, after drinking them a few times, came to the erroneous conclusion that there is no virtue in them."

There is one further flash of fashion to be recorded. Some of the emigrants of the French Revolution lit upon this peaceful neighbourhood as a haven of refuge.

One group settled at Juniper Hall, whose secular and majestic cedars at the foot of Boxhill still refresh the traveller's eye. Here there resided Talleyrand and Madame de Stael, the Duc de Montmorency and M. de Jaucourt, and M. D'Arblay who was courting Fanny Burney. At West Humble were the De Broglies. Another young couple came straight from the church in which they were married to Epsom. Their name was de Gontaut, and she was destined to end as Duchess of Gontaut, Governess of the Children of France. They were delighted with Epsom, where they inhabited a little house "close to the race-course, surrounded by charming country houses. We learned later that our arrival had excited a sensation among the inhabitants of these pretty houses, who were curious to see the French people who had escaped from the disasters of their country, and in the evening peered through our window blinds to see us." The Duchess goes on to describe the races, where the English, she says, lose their habitual phlegm, become active and gay, betting with vivacity and tumult. But this little flock of fugitives soon dispersed again, leaving the faint aroma of a pleasant tradition.

Still, though the waters failed us, a miracle yet remained to be wrought on behalf of Epsom. In the last quarter of the eighteenth century a roystering party at a neighbouring country house founded two races, in two successive years, one for three year old colts and fillies, the other for three year old fillies, and named them gratefully after their host and his house—the Derby and the Oaks. Seldom has a carouse had a more permanent effect. Up to that time Epsom had enjoyed little more

than the ordinary races of a market town. The great
Eclipse, himself, who long lived in Epsom, had run there
in some obscurity. But now horses, some of them
unworthy to draw him in a postchaise, were to earn
immortality by winning on Epsom Downs before
hundreds of thousands of spectators. Parliament was
to adjourn during the ensuing century, not without
debate, to watch the struggle. Ministers and ex-minis-
ters would ride or drive down to the famous race; and in
white hats with blue veils discuss the prospects of their
favourites. Political leaders would give vent to splendid
groans when they realised that they had sold the winner.
In the midst of the Crimean War the result of the Derby
was to be recorded in General Orders. Crowds would
assemble in London, and from London to Epsom, to
watch the still greater crowds returning from the contest.
For a week Epsom would reek of racing. During that
period the eyes of the sporting section of the civilised
world would be turned on the little Surrey town. Many
indeed, who were in no respect sporting, became sporting
for that occasion. It is much the same now. The
Olympian dust is the same, and is still scattered by the
flying horses. The world still admires—not perhaps
with so concentrated a gaze. And all this excitement,
enthusiasm, triumph, whatever you may call it, Epsom
and the universe perhaps owe to an extra magnum of
Lord Derby's choice claret, or a superfluous bottle of
Lord Derby's curious port.

For two weeks, then, or for a part of them, Epsom
races and revels; and recovers during the remaining fifty.
The recovery is less sweet than it was, for what was
once rural is now suburban. But Nature happily, as

we know, is not easily expelled. There are still common land and down, still stately trees and vernal blossom, the nightingales still sing, though it may be to an asylum, the air is still racy and clear.

The time may come when this can no longer be said, when each available inch will be covered by brick or stucco, and when that which cannot be built upon, the still sacred commons, will be surrounded by dun streets of whitey brown houses. Then will be the moment for the resident, who remembers and respects old, or even recent Epsom, to "twitch his mantle blue" and betake himself with his goods and chattels "to fresh woods and pastures new."

EPSOM.

Its History and its Surroundings.

———◆———

CHAPTER I.

———

THE POSITION OF EPSOM
AND A GENERAL DESCRIPTION OF THE
TOWN AND DISTRICT.

T HE town of Epsom, famous alike for its salts and
its races, is situated in the county of Surrey,
just fifteen miles south-west of London. It
lies on the main road to Leatherhead, with the
village of Ewell on the north-east, and Ashtead to the
south-west, and has between it and the edge of the
sprawling suburbs of the metropolis a belt
of pleasant green country quite six miles
wide. Epsom High Street has still that
delightfully sleepy aspect given by great overhanging
roofs, plastered or weatherbeaten red brick walls, and
small paned windows. The London side of the town
has to a great extent thrown off that look of old-world
sobriety, and its shops and houses have to a regrettable
degree assumed the meretricious appearance of a London
suburb. But the old High Street and the modernised

*Situation of
the town.*

portion are, by a fortunate chance, divided sufficiently
for the newer portion to be almost invisible from the old.

About 1711 John Toland wrote, ''When you are on the
top of the Downs, 'tis one of the loveliest
prospects imaginable, to view in the vale
below such an agreeable mixture of trees
and buildings, that a stranger is at a loss
to know whether it be a town in a wood,
or a wood in a town.'' And the statement is to a very
great extent true to-day—Woodcote Park, Durdans,
Woodcote House, Woodcote Grove, and many other
houses having a wealth of splendidly grown trees, while
even the cottages are, in most cases, surrounded by
ample gardens. Even a very unobservant person,
walking up any of the four roads to the Downs, could
scarcely fail to notice this feature. Just behind the
north side of the High Street, are the embankments
of the South Western and the London & Brighton
railways, and beyond it are tranquil green meadows,
broken up by plenty of hedgerow elms and other trees
as far as Horton Manor—a level but well wooded park.
From the midst of the foliage rises the great yellow
brick tower of the Horton Lunatic Asylum, an unwelcome
exchange for Horton Place, the former seat of the
Trotter family. Just where a pleasant lane, now known
as the Hook Road (formerly Kingston Lane), leaves
Epsom in a northerly direction, there has arisen a
cluster of yellow brick, blue slated cottages, so that
instead of passing straight from the town into open
country, with picturesque honeysuckle laden hedges
on either hand, which was possible four or five years
ago, one must be content with an asphalt pavement
and cast iron railings or uninteresting wooden fences
for some distance. The attempt to stem the growth of
London on the part of Queen Elizabeth was futile, and
where so absolute a monarch has failed, under far more
favourable circumstances, it would be of no avail for
the District Council of Epsom to make an attempt.
But luxuriant hedges overgrown with honeysuckle and
travellers' joy are a priceless possession, and to
unthinkingly destroy them is nothing less than criminal.

The profusion of fine trees in the town.

THE "NEW INN," (NOW KNOWN AS "WATERLOO HOUSE") IN HIGH STREET, EPSOM.

In the days of Epsom's popularity as a watering place, this was the largest and most sumptuous Hotel in the town and held the famous ball room.

In Downs Side and other roads there are examples of the delightful appearance of modern houses behind the unsophisticated country hedgerow, quite sufficient to prove the desirability of preserving them in cases where the houses are in no way an ornament to the landscape. In the direction of Ewell, the town spreads itself along the main road for half a mile. There are a miscellaneous collection of shops and private houses, some of them old and picturesque and others quite the reverse. Certainly this entrance to Epsom gives a very erroneous idea of what one may expect in the heart of the town. The approach from Leatherhead over the common and along South Street is, on the other hand, a progression from pure country to large houses in beautiful grounds, and then, without any warning, to the whole of the old High Street. Perhaps the very best view of the place is from the station of the South Western Railway. Below are the red roofs of the town with the clock tower rising from the centre of the street; behind are the groves of trees, hiding nearly all the houses on the south side of the town, and beyond the deep green foliage rise the Downs, those "evergreen mountains of chalk . . . covered with grass finer than Persian carpets," to quote old Toland again.

The prettiest road to Epsom from London is through Tooting and Mitcham, then by a turning to the right by Mitcham station, one may join the main road from Wimbledon at the little village of Morden, whose inn, the "George," was quite important in coaching days, having been one of the hostelries where the Horsham coach changed horses. Beyond Morden, the road is undulating, and on account of the magnificent elms which line the hedges for most of the way to Ewell, it is an exceptionally pretty highway at all seasons of the year.

CHAPTER II.

CONCERNING EPSOM FROM THE
EARLIEST TIMES
TO THE PRESENT DAY.

W HEN the greater part of Surrey was covered
with forests, and at the time of the Roman
occupation, Epsom probably was not.
Although many traces of Roman work have
been found in the neighbourhood, at Chessington, at
Ewell, at Ashtead, on the Downs, and elsewhere, Epsom
itself has yielded practically nothing. And this is not
surprising, for it is just off the Stane Street—generally
known as the Ermyn Street north of Dorking—and the
military outposts were unlikely to choose such a spot as
that occupied by the town, in those days doubtless full
of impenetrable woods and thickets, and in part, of a
very marshy character.

Canon Isaac Taylor says that Epsom is a corruption
of the Anglo-Saxon *Ebesham,* the " home
of Ebe," with the suffix *-ham* obscured.
According to Brayley it has come to its
present form through the successive stages
of *Ebbisham, Ebesham,* and *Epsham.* Authorities seem
to agree upon its derivation from Ebba's ham, home,
or dwelling—Ebba being an Anglo-Saxon feminine
name ; but it is not nearly so certain who Ebba was.
John Toland, whose description of Epsom is quoted
elsewhere, says that the kingdom of the South Saxons
continued in the posterity of Ælla, its founder, to

Derivation of the Name

Ethelwolf, the first Christian King of the South Saxons, whose Queen was Ebba, of whom Thomas Rudborne, who wrote in the time of Henry III in his *Manuscript Chronicle* in the Cottonian Library (Nero A. 17) says, *Regina vero nomine Ebbe in sua, id est Wiccianorum provincia, fuerat baptizata. Erat autem Gustridi filia, fratris Ruheri, qui ambo cum suo populo Christiani fuerunt.*

[The Queen, whose real name was Ebba, had been baptised in her own province, *i.e.,* that of the South Saxons. She was, moreover, the daughter of Gustridus, the brother of Ruberus, both of whom in common with their people had been Christians.]

Æthelbert was the first Christian King in England, and Edilwalch seems to have been the first King of the South Saxons to accept Christianity. Toland's reference to Ethelwolf is therefore quite inaccurate.

Ebba is also believed to have been a Northumbrian Princess, Camden stating that she was the daughter of Ethelfred (? Ethelfrith), and that about 630 she had such a character for sanctity that she was canonized, and had several churches dedicated to her, commonly called St. Ebba's.

The Venerable Bede mentions Ebba as Abbess of Coldingham in Berwickshire, who, with her nuns, mutilated their faces in order to preserve themselves from violation by the Danes, who, notwithstanding, burnt them all with the abbey. St. Abb's Head was named after the saintly Abbess who built a nunnery on the verge of the promentary, a few foundation stones of which are still discernible. Coldingham Priory was consecrated to St. Cuthbert, St. Mary, and *St. Ebba.* It was a famous establishment right up to the time of Cromwell, the office of Prior of Coldingham having in 1514 been held by David Home, brother of the Earl of Home. There is, however, no authority for stating that this Ebba ever married a Saxon king.

Toland states that on the site of Epsom Court—now Epsom Court Farm—was the original Saxon seat, " in old writings is likewise called Ebbysham-place ; now only a great name, and nothing more to be seen, but an oblong square area rais'd higher than the other ground, on the south-east of the house. Abundance of wrought stone, of Roman bricks and tiles are often dug up about the farm."

To-day Epsom Court Farm shows no traces of any Saxon dwelling. The house is no more than fifty years old, but an isolated little cottage just beyond the barns, probably forming a part of the very old range of farm buildings, is old enough to have contracted the usual tale of Queen Elizabeth having stopped there one night. It is a very picturesque little place with huge oak beams in the gable ends, a prominent projecting chimney stack and leaded windows.

It may also be mentioned that there has been another suggestion for the derivation of the name Epsom from an intermitting spring in the chalk, called the Earth bourn or bore. This even in comparatively recent years used to flow down the Worple Road and across the meadows by the present Parade and flood the fields at the lower end of Church Street where the Town Hall, the Institute, and other new buildings stand, and at the present time it is carried off by drains. In Lye's Saxon Dictionary the word " Ebbe " is translated " an Ebb," *recessus aquarium*.

Before the Norman Conquest the manor of Epsom

Epsom at the Compilation of the Domesday Book.
belonged to the abbot of Chertsey. The Domesday Book records that, " The abbot holds *Ebesham,* which in the time of King Edward was assessed at 33 hides ; now at 11 hides. The arable land consists of 17 carucates. There is 1 carucate in demesne ; and thirty-four villeins, and four bordars, have 17 carucates. There are two churches ; and six bondmen and two mills valued at 10 shillings ; and 24 acres of meadow. The wood yields 20 hogs. In the time of King Edward it was valued at 20l., now at 17l." Concerning the two churches mentioned, Salmon, in his " Antiquities of Surrey " says, " I am apt to think here have been two parishes laid together, one at Woodcote or Durdans, which the convent had united with Ebbisham before the Conquest." One church was probably found sufficient for the united

parishes, the Woodcote church having disappeared, and no traces of it are discoverable to-day. Woodcote and Epsom were considered as practically separate places even as late as 1679, for in that year it is recorded in the court rolls of the manor of Ebbisham that it was presented to be the custom to elect two constables, one for Epsom and one for Woodcote, and that the custom prevailed with respect to the other officers.

Where the two mills mentioned in the Domesday Survey were, it is impossible to say, and there is not sufficient water in the parish to turn one. They could not have been windmills, for the earliest mention of them in this country is during the reign of Richard I, when it is believed that they were introduced from the East. In 1295 a windmill is alluded to as standing at Walton-on-the-Hill. "They were probably," says Pownall, "cattle or ban mills, that is mills at which the vassals were obliged to grind their corn, for which they paid toll in kind."

Early in the 12th century the abbot of Chertsey received a license to shut up his park at Epsom whenever he chose. He also had all the beasts found in it, while Edward I in 1285 granted a charter of free-warren in the manor of Epsom. What "all the beasts" implied may be inferred from the fact that the last wolf in Great Britain was killed in Scotland as late as 1680, and in place of the sheep and cattle one may see grazing to-day in Woodcote Park, there were doubtless wild cats, wild boars, wild red deer, the wild bull with its white mane, and the marten, whose fur was only exceeded in value by sable. These, with numbers of smaller animals, were still to be found in secluded spots in this country in the time of Charles II.

Purchased by Henry VIII in 1537, the manor of Ebbisham passed through many hands— to mention them all would merely be wearisome. Among the more important owners were Sir Nicholas Carew in Henry VIII's reign, Edward D'Arcy—one of the grooms of the privy bedchamber of Queen Elizabeth, Richard Evelyn of Woodcote, John Parkhurst in 1707, and Sir Joseph Mawbey, High Sheriff for Surrey in 1757, who

The Descent of the Manor.

obtained the manor by purchase. There was also the manor of Horton and another called Bruttgave, Brettgrave, or Bruttegrave. This last manor is very obscure, for it is quite impossible to locate its position to-day. In the reign of Edward IV. the manor of Brettegrave was connected with the Merston family who owned Horton Manor, and there is therefore every reason to believe that the manors of Horton and Brettgrave were merged into one.

The year 1618 saw the discovery of the mineral wells at Epsom, and from that date the obscure village, with practically no history worth recording, immediately became famous in England, and shortly afterwards throughout Europe. By the middle of the eighteenth century the town had lost its popularity, and the place seems to have settled into the habitual calm it presents to-day, only rendered more impressive by contrast with the excitement, the crowds, the dust and noise of race days. Epsom is stated to have formerly had a market on Fridays, but this has long been discontinued.

Just before the construction of the first railway to **Coaching Days.** Epsom, the High Street showed more signs of activity, for there was the daily excitement of the arrivals and departures of the coaches. At 9 o'clock in the morning, the Horsham coach arrived on its way to London, driven by Bob Whittle, the fastest whip on the road. "Little Robert," as he was affectionately termed by his brother drivers, passed through Epsom again at 5 in the evening. The following list will give some idea of the daily coach service.

To LONDON.		Starting from
8 a.m.	Hunt's 2 horse coach - - -	The Spread Eagle, Epsom.
8.20 ,,	Broad's 4 ,, ,, - - -	Dorking.
9 ,,	"Little Robert" 4 horse coach -	Horsham.
10 ,,	4 horse coach driven by Kirby -	Guildford.
10.20 ,,	Matthew Holden's 4 horse coach	Dorking.
2 p.m.	"The Sovereign" 4 horse coach	Worthing ⎱ on alternate days.
3 ,,	"The Comet" 4 horse coach -	Bognor. ⎰
4.30 ,,	Walker's 4 horse coach - -	Dorking.

HIGH STREET, EPSOM SHOWING THE OLD WATCH HOUSE AND SIGNBOARD OF THE KING'S HEAD HOTEL

From an Engraving published about seventy years ago.

11 a.m.	Walker's 4 horse coach (driven by the proprietor).	-	to Dorking
11.30 ,,	"The Comet" - - -	-	to Worthing and Bognor.
5 p.m.	4 horse coach driven by Kirby	-	to Guildford.
5 ,,	"Little Robert" 4 horse coach	-	to Horsham.
5 ,,	Matthew Holden's 4 horse coach		to Dorking.
6 ,,	Broad's 4 horse coach	- -	to ,,
6.30 ,,	Hunt's 2 ,, ,,	- -	to Epsom.

Of the Epsom coach, a publication of 1825 states that: "The civil deportment and obliging attention of the proprietor, Mr. Hunt, greatly enhance the accommodation afforded by his coach, and entitle him to the patronage and support of the inhabitants." The expense of the journey by coach often induced people of limited means to walk to and from London, while the gentry often rode on horseback. For cross country journeys, off the coach routes, it was always necessary to post.

In 1848 a branch line from Croydon was built, having
The advent of the Railways. its terminus at Epsom. In the Bill authorising its construction, it seems to have been intended as a "pneumatic" railway. But it was evidently considered impractical, for the first and every subsequent train on this line has been driven by steam. The railway was eventually continued to Leatherhead, and either before or shortly afterwards the loop line from Wimbledon connecting Epsom with Waterloo Bridge Station (its original name) was built.

The year 1848 was a sad one for Epsom, for not only did the picturesque coaches begin to disappear, but the quaint little Watch House in the High Street was pulled down, and in its place was built the present clock tower. Stocks stood by the old structure, and these disappeared at its demolition, and no one knows what became of them. The new building is of red and yellow brick
The Clock Tower and Pond. with ornamental stonework here and there, and would be an ornament to the town, if it were not surmounted by a senseless gilded Chinese cupola, suggestive of the top storey of a pagoda. If the architect had copied the

little classical bell turrets still to be seen on so many of the old market houses of this country, the building would have never been spoken of with contempt, and it is still possible to effect the alteration.

It was not until 1854 that the pond which had occupied the centre of the High Street was filled in, and another picturesque feature removed. The Local Board of Health had been instituted in 1850, and this was one of its early activities. The pond was insanitary, no doubt, but it would have been possible to keep it pure, and it could scarcely have been considered a hindrance to traffic.

The first Board of Health at Epsom. From a printed paper, dated 1850, I have been enabled to give the following particulars of the first Board of Health.

ELECTION OF LOCAL BOARD OF HEALTH
FOR THE
EPSOM DISTRICT—SURREY,
1850.

WHEREAS by an ORDER of HER MAJESTY the QUEEN in council, made on the 9th day of March of 1850, it was ordered and directed, that from and after that date, the Public Health Act, 1848, and every part thereof, except Section 50, should be applied to, and be in force within the district of Parish Epsom, in the County of Surrey.

Names of members elected.

Robert John Phillip Jaquet, 189 votes, Gentleman, Ivy Cottage, Epsom.

Alexander Wood, 183 votes, Gentleman, Priam Cottage, Epsom.

Thomas Tompson, 186 votes, Draper, High St., Epsom.

William Harsant, 236 votes, Chemist and Druggist, High St., Epsom.

Lawrence Langlands, 173 votes, Builder, High St., Epsom.

John Bailey, 182 votes, Draper, High St., Epsom.

George Stilwell, 184 votes, Surgeon, Church St., Epsom.

Sir Richard Digby Neave, 179 votes, Baronet, Pit Place, Epsom.

Edward Richard Northey, 172 votes, Esquire, Woodcote, Epsom.

Given under my hand, this Ninth day of May, 1850,

WILLIAM EVEREST.

HIGH STREET, EPSOM.
Showing the Clock Tower and Waterloo House.

John Bailey, the draper mentioned in this list, was

In
Early
Victorian
Times.

commonly known as the " Epsom Banker," for about this period his shop in Waterloo House, now under the name of Oldridge, was the only one of any pretensions in the whole neighbourhood, and his customers came from astonishing distances. So thronged used the shop to become with ladies purchasing the loud patterned and crude coloured Early Victorian drapery then in fashion, that it was quite common to hear people exclaim, " I have been at Bailey's over an hour, and can't get served ! "

The last old gentleman to give up the bob-wig or queue in Epsom was a Mr. Storey, who lived at Cromwell Lodge in Church Street about the year 1838.

About this period, too, the last of the old trees in the High Street had not been cut down. From the shop now occupied by Chamberlain, the baker, to near the passage way leading to the South Western Station, there extended a row of polled limes or elms. In course of time all but two opposite the baker's shop were cleared away. For a time the two veterans, sawn down to stumps, survived, supporting between them a wooden seat where the occupant of the shop facing them was wont to smoke his pipe in his spare moments. At last these disappeared, and now from end to end of the High Street the pavements are bare.

The newest shops are at the east end of the town,

The Old
Inns.

while some of those in the old portion of the High Street still retain their small-paned windows of delightful picturesqueness. Waterloo House, originally the " New Inn," and the old building now used as a shop by Young the grocer, also an inn in former days, are undoubtedly the most beautiful of all the old buildings in the High Street, while the inns which still keep to their calling have nearly all of them a quaint and interesting aspect. The grocer's shop just mentioned is especially interesting on account of its wide staircase and heavy turned balusters. Most prominent among the inns owing to the open space in front of it is the " Spread Eagle." Its

walls are cream washed, its chimney stacks are solid
and prominent, and its tiled roofs are in some portions
velvety with moss, In a recess which might have been
a blocked up window, in the upper floor, hangs the old
swing sign, very black with age, but still showing the
outline of an eagle. Through the archway in the front
of the building one may catch a glimpse of the extensive

THE "SPREAD EAGLE" HOTEL,
In High Street, Epsom, one of the famous old inns of the town.

stabling at the back. It is, however, scarcely sufficient
to meet the demands made upon it during race weeks.
The main staircase of the hotel has a fine old balustrade
with a wide moulded handrail and heavy newel posts.
The large room used for public meetings has a door

C2

with richly moulded panels. It is painted now, and
has been pierced with a square hole for hearing masonic
passwords.

Opposite the clock tower, on the south side of the
High Street, stands the King's Head. Its signboard
has gone, its frontage on the street has been considerably
altered, but the core of the building remains practically
the same. From the stable yard, the building seems
scarcely touched since the time of Pepys, old red brick
gables and chimneys rising above one another in
delightful fashion.

Where the new erection known as "The Shades"
now stands, there was formerly a small house where
the post boys ate and slept in uncomfortably close
quarters, and what is now the entrance hall of the hotel
was originally open to the road in front. At the back
of this open space a gallery ran across the first floor.
In 1838 the present assembly room was built over the
space, and the room at the back of the gallery was
thrown into it. The new and the old work are easily
discernible from the exterior, the new portion being
slate roofed. In this Assembly Room most of the public
meetings of the town, including the County Ball, were
held before the present Public Hall was built. It
is reached by a wide modern staircase, but in other
parts of the building there are no fewer than three
other flights of stairs. These are rather dark and
narrow, with plenty of oak beams covered by many
thicknesses of wallpaper, and are far more suggestive
of Epsom's famous days. The stabling here, as at the
"Spread Eagle," is very extensive. From this yard
there is a good view of a long avenue of limes in the
garden of Ashley House—that austere classic-fronted
house in Ashley Road, the former residence of a
Mrs. Ashley, who gave her name to the house and
road. The trees are well-grown, but they are not old
enough to have seen the days of Queen Anne.

The "Albion," formerly known as the "Coffee House,"
at the south-west end of the High Street is an old
establishment, smaller than those just mentioned, but
it has a very old-fashioned aspect, and is conspicuous

by its large projecting upper window. About sixty years ago this inn was kept by Mr. Thomas Baker, a retired worthy of Doctor's Commons. This gentleman produced such a high-class tone about the inn, that it was playfully nick-named "The House of Lords," while the magistrates' courts were for many years held in the large front room on the first floor. But more rustic than any is the little "Magpie" Inn in South Street close by, with its boarded walls and its signboard suspended from a pollard elm. Next door to the "Magpie" stands an old-world grocer's shop, whose two capacious and at the same time very quaint windows are always arranged in the typical fashion of the country, generally with two great white bladders of lard flanked by Dutch cheeses as the most prominent features. On the pavement outside is a post with a ring attached for fastening up horses. On the other side and opposite end of South Street is a low and quaint wooden building with mossy tiled roofs known as the "Queen's Head." This is undoubtedly the inn referred to in Larwood and Hotten's "History of Signboards:" "At New Inn Lane (now South Street) Harlow painted a front and back view of Queen Charlotte to settle a bill he had run up; he imitated Sir Thomas Lawrence's style, and signed it 'T. L.,' Greek Street, Soho. When Lawrence heard this, he got in a terrible rage and said, if Harlow were not a scoundrel, he would kick him from one street's end to the other; upon which Harlow very coolly remarked, that when Sir Thomas should make up his mind to it, he hoped he would choose a short street." This incident occurred through a difference between Harlow and Sir Thomas Lawrence, P.R.A., in whose studio he worked—the caricature signboard being Harlow's foolish revenge. George Henry Harlow was born in St. James's Street, London, in 1787, and died at the early age of thirty-two. His portrait by himself may be seen in the National Portrait Gallery. The man who has twice painted up the signboard of the "Queen's Head," states that on one occasion the board was scraped bare to the wood, so that there is now no possibility of restoring the original portrait.

Much of the charm of old Epsom depends on the lowness of its houses—they seldom exceed two storeys in height with dormers in the roof, but those who have been responsible for the new buildings in the town have either failed to realise this, or other motives have prompted them to build up to four storeys, giving the new work a prominence which even time will be unable to eradicate, and interfering to a most unwelcome extent with the general roof line. Fortunately this new work is in red brick and of good design towards the street, but there is one exception—a yellow brick structure, full of mahogany and frosted glass.

The New Buildings.

The post office, in Tudor style, the new bank close by with its curved projecting windows and heavy wooden dentelle work, and the group of shops extending from the High Street to the London & Brighton Station are welcome, and would be all that could be desired if they were a storey lower. The new bank opposite the " Spread Eagle " is especially noteworthy from its bearing a certain resemblance in style with Waterloo House, reproducing in new material the simplicity and charm of the old building.

The Public Hall occupies a prominent position at the junction of Church Street with High Street and Station Road. The site was an awkwardly shaped one and this must be taken as an excuse for its most unfortunate appearance from every position except from immediately in front. It is built in classic style of terra-cotta, with pilasters by the windows and doors, and with a heavy pediment above. But the flamboyant front does not seem to belong in any way to the plain sides of the hall, as though it were intended to hide them with other buildings on either side. So little respect is paid to these side walls that they are generally covered with advertisements; and now advertisements have been mentioned, it is impossible to refrain from expressing astonishment at the extent with which the town is disfigured with posters and hoardings. They are to be seen in Church Street, in East Street, in the High Street, and in South Street

The Public Hall.

in such quantities that one longs for some influential local committee capable of saving so quaint a town from the tattered grip of the advertiser.

Close to the Public Hall in Church Street stands the Technical Institute. It has a red brick and terra cotta frontage, but will be immensely improved when the adjoining space is built upon and its bare untreated side hidden. The Institute of earlier days may still be seen in the High Street—a pathetic sight, its classic stucco front looking very dilapidated and its sides plastered with posters. Fifty years ago this building held a fair library and reading room, but through the growth of an element among some of the members contrary to the proper conduct of the Institution, it was allowed to fall through, the books it contained being sold by auction.

On the opposite side of the street further east are some new shops, standing on the site of "Rabbit-hutch Row"—a collection of low and unpretentious wooden shops.

From the High Street the town scatters itself over the gently rising ground in the direction of the Downs. Church Street, originally one of the Parades of Stuart times, is still a charming road. With the exception of two or three new shops and cottages near the town there is nothing to disturb its old world calm, and nearly every house is worthy of some study. Richly ornamented doorways, curiously massive chimneys, steep tiled roofs, old pebble dash walls, and little dormer windows are to be seen on every side. A specially attractive spot is near St. Martin's Church. Here the road is narrow, and there are plenty of tall trees on both sides. The "Old King's Head," a very picturesque little inn with a bright red sign and a little wooden outside table, faces the church, with the long low red-tiled roof of "The Farm" showing above the garden wall ; opposite are the large gates of Pit Place with its supercilious lions surmounting the pillars on either side.

Not far from here Church Street becomes the Burgh Heath Road, and with modern houses on either side for a short distance goes right up to the Downs.

Downs Road, formerly known as Walnut Tree Road, leads out of the end of Church Street. It is fairly high and is much more open than nearer the town, while the architecture of its new houses is very attractive. Ashley Road may be reached by a turning out of Downs Road. Here every house is modern but not quite so recent as those in the road just left. Of the four routes to the Downs this has the easiest gradient. The Worple Road from Church Street cuts through the Ashley Road and then runs right into Woodcote End, between fine old red brick walls overhung by the huge elms of Woodcote Grove.

From Woodcote End runs Chalk Lane—formerly written Creken or Cricker Lane—a very beautiful shady road passing the grounds of Durdans and giving a very good view of the house. A footpath a little higher than this point goes through a pleasant meadow and comes out into the Ashley Road.

Under the shadow of the Downs, between the Ashley and the Downs Roads is situated the Cemetery. It is very well kept and is full of well-grown evergreen trees. The first interment was in 1871.

The East side of the town is less interesting than the other portions, being of modern growth, although East Street itself has some buildings which have been there for nearly two centuries. The old almshouses built by John Levingstone, the notorious apothecary, were pulled down about forty years ago and were subsequently re-built in red brick and slate. Alexandra Road, running up towards Epsom College and the Downs, has in it the Cottage Hospital, a low gabled building designed by Mr. J. R. Harding, with very good views over the town owing to the general elevation of the road. It was· erected as a memorial of Queen Victoria's Jubilee in 1887, and was opened in 1889 by Princess Mary, Duchess of Teck.

Church Road is parallel with Church Street, and Station Road leads past the London and Brighton Station.

It is in the memories of those still living that the land between Church Street and Ashley Road, immediately at the back of the High Street, was chiefly covered with cornfields, and the houses in what is now known as the Parade were connected by a very primitive footpath. It is now an asphalted passage with a high fence on one side. Two or three of the cottages here have delightful gardens, in summer time, a wilderness of bright flowers, while a little turning close by is common-place enough until its numerous laburnums fill it with a blaze of yellow. Springtime is delicious in Epsom, for its large and well-kept gardens fill the roads with the scents of early blossoms to an astonishing extent. Out of the south-west end of the High Street runs West Hill, leading to Stamford Green and the Common, passing Hookfield, the residence of Mr. Basil Braithwaite, on the left, and on the right Christchurch Room, West Hill House, and overlooking Clay Hill Green, the pretty little Infant School founded by the late Miss Trotter.

Epsom College stands well outside the town in the direction of the downs, the red brick buildings, with their numerous chimney stacks, being one of the conspicuous landmarks near the town. The college was founded by Dr. Propert as recently as 1851, and the buildings were opened in 1855 by Prince Albert, who was accompanied by King Edward VII, then a boy of fourteen years old.

On October 10th in the same year the first term commenced, the number of scholars being nearly a hundred, all of them sons of medical men. The school was not restricted to those whose fathers were in the medical profession, except so far as concerned boys who were on the foundation : that all the original scholars were doctors' sons was therefore unintentional.

The first head-master was the Rev. Robinson Thornton, now Archdeacon of Middlesex. In 1870 he was succeeded by Dr. West, and in 1885 came the Rev. W. C. Woods' brief tenure of the head-mastership. He died in 1888 to the great regret of all, and was succeeded by the Rev. T. N. Hart-Smith, who is the present head-master.

King Edward again visited the college as Prince of Wales in 1895, accompanied by the Princess of Wales

and the Princess Victoria, to lay the foundation stone of
the lower school. The chapel was built in 1857, and
has been enlarged by the addition of the East end and
transepts.

For the first twenty-eight years all the boys were
under the personal care of the headmaster; they are
now divided into four houses under the names of
Carr, Forest, Propert, and Granville. The building
devoted to the medical pensioners who used to reside
in the college has been gradually converted into
masters' houses, for the new pensioners are no longer
housed in the school buildings.

In gymnastics Epsom College is above the average
school standard, and it possesses in addition an efficient
rifle corps and fire brigade. For thirty years or more
the college has had its natural history society, which
publishes its proceedings annually.

' The extensive grounds of the school give ample space
for the numerous games played by the boys.

CHAPTER III.

IN WHICH AN ATTEMPT IS MADE TO
DESCRIBE EPSOM IN
THE SEVENTEENTH CENTURY.

O N a certain tombstone, in a certain churchyard,
were written the lines,

> " Here lies I and my three daughters,
> Died from drinking the Cheltenham waters,
> If we had stuck to Epsom salts,
> We shouldn't be lying in these cold vaults,'

and it would not be easy to find a more fitting testimony
to the excellent properties of the famous salts.

The chance discovery of the mineral spring on the
common has made Epsom a household name throughout
Europe and wherever English is spoken. But for that
fortuitous circumstance, Epsom would be as little known
as Chipstead or Headley, or any other remote Surrey
village.

The man to whom Epsom owes so much is, according
to " Fuller's Worthies," Henry Wicker or
Wickes, who, during the very dry summer
of 1618, discovered on the common a small
hole filled with water. He is said to have
dug it out larger and then to have brought his cattle to
drink it. To his astonishment the cows, without exception, refused to touch the water. This led to some
considerable talk ; a further examination of the hole
was made, aad the healing nature of the waters was
discovered, at first for external sores, and eventually
for internal use as an aperient and purifier of the blood.

Discovery
of the
Waters.

Brayley, who mentions this account, also adds that the exact date of the discovery is uncertain. "It has been stated," he says, "that towards the close of the reign of Queen Elizabeth, the waters of a pond on the common, half a mile westward of the village, were found to be serviceable in the cure of ulcers and other disorders; and after the accession of James the First, some physician, having heard of the virtues attributed to this water, visited the place, and found on examination that it was impregnated with a bitter purging salt, which was then erroneously termed calcareous nitre, but which has been since named (from its known composition) sulphate of magnesia, though still, in common parlance, called Epsom salt." I have quoted this account at length as it is necessary to be authoritative on so important a matter.

Whatever the year of actual discovery, we know definitely that the spring began to get a reputation for its healing properties, bringing strangers to test its powers, so that about 1621 the owner of the estate who was fortunate enough to possess the spring, surrounded it with a wall, and built what has generally been called a "shed" for the protection of invalids. Another twenty years passed, and the fame of the Spa had extended to Germany, France, and most of the European countries, bringing many continental persons of distinction to Epsom.

Aubrey gives the date of the discovery as 1639-40, and he drank of the waters in 1654. But the third Lord North writes of the wells as famous in 1645. In his "Forest of Varieties," published in that year, he claims for himself the credit of having first made known the Tonbridge and Epsom waters "to the citizens of London and the king's people"—1618 is therefore the more probable date.

By the year 1668 it was a common occurrence for doctors to advise a visit to Epsom, for in the Domestic State Papers of June 29 in that year we read, "Chatham Dockyard. John Owen to Pepys. I beg leave of absence for 12 days, being afflicted with . . . and advised to drink Epsom waters." In the following

August there is another entry : " Chatham Dock. Ph. Pett to the Navy Commissioners. I beg leave of absence for a fortnight through ill health, being advised by my physician to drink Epsom waters."

About this time also the dissolute Court of Charles II repaired to rural little Epsom in such numbers, attracting most of the fashionable folk of London, that in the *London Gazette* for June 19th, 1684, there appeared an announcement that " the post will go every day, to and fro betwixt London and Epsom, during the season for drinking the waters." The season was in the early summer, so that the country was then greenest, and the birds had not ceased their song.

About 1690, when it is stated that John Parkhurst *Improvements at the Wells.* was lord of the manor, prodigious and astonishing changes were brought about at the wells. A ballroom quite seventy feet in length was erected together with a number of other rooms for accommodating the throng of gentry, and a piece of land was surrounded by a brick wall with a freestone coping. This wall survived for a considerably longer period than the ballroom, for though dilapidated it was still standing in 1825. Mr. Parkhurst seems also to have been responsible for planting the long row of elms and limes leading from the London road through the town and branching out afterwards in two or three directions. These trees afterwards became very ornamental, and extended down New Inn Lane through the town and halfway to Ewell, but in the first few years of the nineteenth century they were nearly all cut down by Sir Joseph Mawbey, then lord of the manor, and the timber sold for a considerable sum. For this outrageous piece of work no language is too strong, and there was evidently some feeling at the time, for we read that Sir Joseph promised to give £200 towards a new market-house, and to make the market toll free for seven years. In 1825 this had not been done, and Sir Joseph had long been gathered to his fathers. At the same time as the extensive building operations at the wells, a similar activity prevailed in the town, and inns, coffee-houses, and lodgings were multiplied with astonishing rapidity.

The greatest wonder of all was the New Inn, built about 1690, still standing in the High Street, but for some trivial reason labelled "Waterloo House." At the time of its construction it was reputed to be the largest establishment of its kind in England, and was probably regarded

The "New Inn."

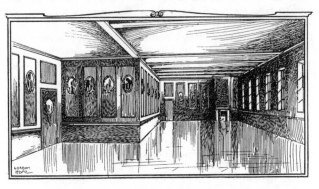

From the position marked with a star in the Plan, this is the aspect of the room before it was divided in the centre. The candle sconces are added in the positions they would have been likely to occupy.

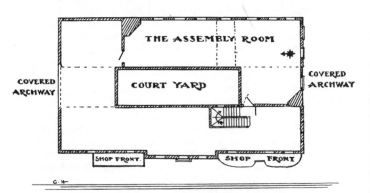

SKETCH PLAN OF THE UPPER FLOOR OF THE "NEW INN,"
Showing position of the Assembly Room and of the entrances to the Courtyard.

with as much awe by the natives as the hotel on Crow-
borough Beacon in Sussex is imposing to the yokels of
that sparsely populated district. The " New Inn " was
kept by a Mrs. Wright, and
is so little altered that it is
possible to give some idea of
the place under her manage-
ment. The building, as I
have mentioned before, is
constructed of a beautiful
warm coloured red brick,
with facings of that soft
chalk stone so largely used
at that period. A wide gable
end faces the street, the
eaves are ornamented with
heavy wooden dentelle work
and mouldings painted some
colour approximating white.
The roof is covered with
ancient tiles of the loveliest
umber shades, where they
are not green with moss.
A long narrow courtyard
occupied the centre of the
building, so that coaches
were able to drive in through
the archway at one side and
out at the other. Only a
very superficial glance at
the exterior of the building
will suffice to show the
position of these archways
now blocked up and covered
with stucco. At the present

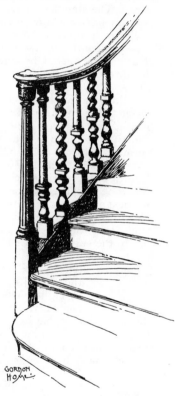

A PORTION OF THE STAIRCASE IN THE
" NEW INN,"

At the western end of the building.

time the ground floor is so
much cut up by the draper's
shop at one end, and hidden with old furniture at the
other, that there is little to remind one of the original
use of the place, but on the first floor is the long
dancing saloon or assembly room, divided near the

centre, it is true, but still sufficiently itself for obtaining an excellent idea of the background of so many fashionable frivolities. From a most careful examination, I have been able to make the drawing reproduced here. The staircases have fine balustrades, which may possibly have come from Nonsuch Palace.

About sixty years or more ago, the Assembly Room was frequently the scene of cockfights. They are clearly remembered by one old inhabitant of Epsom, the favourite time for the contests being Sunday afternoon.

A little earlier than this, a travelling company converted the room into a theatre. One of the announcement bills, dated January 12th, 1829, is still in existence. The title of the play was "Speed the Plough, or the Farmer's Glory." The bill states that the theatre was "at the old Assembly Room, tastefully decorated with neat and appropriate scenery." The proprietor adds that "he proposes representing the choicest plays of our best authors, delineated by a company of performers whose acknowledged ability added to their regular conduct in their private capacity he trusts will entitle him to the support and patronage of the liberal-minded inhabitants."

Pepys visited Epsom in 1667, and in his diary under the date July 14, he writes, "To Epsum, by eight o'clock, to the well; where much company. And to the towne to the King's Head; and hear that my Lord Buckhurst and Nelly lodged at the next house, and Sir Charles Sedley with them: and keep a merry house."

Pepys at Epsom.

This house, next door to the "King's Head," where Nelly, more commonly Nell Gwynne, stayed, is still standing, the ground floor being utilised as a grocer's shop. Unfortunately the interior has been altered too much to leave anything suggestive of that time, and one is forced to be content with knowing that the court favourite occupied the two little bay-windowed rooms overlooking the street, one of them being used as a bedroom and the other as a sitting-room. During a comparatively recent alteration,

Nell Gwynne.

a very small doorway was discovered in one of the walls of the left-hand room as one faces the building. This might have been used as a secret entrance or exit, but it is entirely covered up with plaster and wall papers now, so that it is impossible to examine it without having the wall pulled to pieces.

NELL GWYNNE,
One of Epsom's famous visitors.
From the Painting by Sir Peter Lely in the National Portrait Gallery.

On July 25th, 1663, Pepys writes, " . . . Towards the evening we bade them adieu ! and took horse ; being resolved that we would go to Epsom. When we come

D

there we could hear of no lodging, the town so full ; but which was better, I went toward Ashted, and there we got a lodging in a little hole we could not stand upright in. While supper was getting I walked up and down behind my cosen Pepy's house that was, which I find comes little short of what I took it to be when I was a little boy.

"26th (Lord's day). Up and to the Wells, where a great store of citizens, which was the greatest part of the company, though there were some others of better quality. Thence I walked to Mr. Minnes's house,* and thence to Durdan's, and walked within the Court Yard and to the Bowling-green, where I have seen so much mirth in my time ; but now no family in it, (my Lord Barkeley, whose it is, being with his family at London.) Then rode through Epsom, the whole town over, seeing the various companys that were there walking ; which was very pleasant to see how they are there without knowing what to do, but only in the morning to drink waters. But Lord ! to see how many I met there of citizens, that I could not have thought to have seen there ; that they had ever had it in their heads or purses to go down thither."

Charles II often visited Epsom, dining on one occasion at Durdans, only just built from the materials of Nonsuch Palace. Tradition says that he built for Nell Gwynne the stabling in Church Street, opposite St. Martin's, now known as "The Farm," and partly converted into a private house. The age of the place certainly supports this belief. It consists of one long line of buildings under one unbroken gabled roof. The walls are a strange medley of red brick and great blocks of chalk covered with close growing ivy, while the roof tiles are a beautiful subdued red. In the portion still used as a stable, the solid oak beams in the roof may be seen. These are now so hardened with age, that in a fire which broke out in one of the loose boxes a few months ago, they merely charred on the surface, and were practically the means of saving this relic of Stuart times from destruction.

*Horton Manor.

About the year 1711 John Toland came to live at
Woodcote, and while there he wrote a long
account of Epsom to a lady he addresses
as "Eudoxa." I have taken the following
extracts from the letter as it appears in the
volume published in 1726, entitled "A collection of
several pieces of Mr. Toland."

Toland's Account of Epsom.

" MADAM,
. . . Epsom, a village in the County of
Surrey, much frequented for its most healthy Air and
excellent mineral Waters, is distant about fourteen
Italian miles from London Bridge, and twelve from
Fox-hall. It is deliciously situated in a warm even
bottom antiently called Flower-dale, between the finest
Downs in the world on one side (taking their name from
the village of Banstead seated on their very ridge) and
certain clay hills on the other side, which are variously
chequered with woods and groves of oak, ash, elm,
and beech, with both the poplars, the intoxicating yew,
and the florid white-beam. The wyche-tree, the withy,
the horn-beam, the bird-feeding quicken-tree, and the
correcting birch, are not wanting. I need not mention
the numberless copses of hazel, thorn, holly, maple,
and other trees and shrubs of dwarfish growth, that
agreeably diversify all this country : nor that, for the
most part, they are amorously claspt in the twining
embraces of ivy and honey-suckles. The Downs, being
covered with grass finer than Persian Carpets, and
perfum'd with wild thyme and juniper, run thirty miles
in length, tho' under different appellations, from Croydon
to Farnham : and for sheep-walks, riding, hunting,
raceing, shooting, with games of most sorts for exercise
of the body or recreation of the mind, and a perpetual
chain of villages within a mile of each other beneath,
they are nowhere else to be parallel'd. The form of
this our village, as seen from thence, is exactly semi-
circular ; beginning with a Church and ending with a
Palace : or lest our stile here shou'd offend you, Madam,
it has a Palace for its head and a Church for its tail.
Mr. Whistler's far conspicuous grove makes, as it

were, a beautiful knot in the middle : as the road from thence to Woodcote-green, may be called Midway Street. Epsom never misses of the Eastern or Western Sun and is about a mile in length ; the area, within the bending of the bow or half-moon, being a spacious plain of cornfields, sown with every grain, and opening full to the downs. To these ever-green mountains of chalk you may out of every house insensibly ascend, without as much as a hedge to obstruct the air or the passage. Indeed the risings are many times so easy, that you find yourself got to the top, without perceiving that you were mounting. From the circumference of the semicircle there branch out two or three pleasant lanes, being the extremities of the roads which lead to the town, from the slow declivities of the neighbouring hills. These are prefer'd to the principal street by such as are lovers of silence and retirement ; and are known by the names of Clay-hill, New-inn-lane,* and Woodcote-green, in which last place your humble servant has his hermitage. There are other alleys and outlets of meaner note. Among them I don't reckon the avenue leading up the hill to Durdans, the Palace I just now mention'd ; nor yet Hudson's lane†, which I remember for the sake of Epsom-Court, that antient Saxon Seat (long since converted into a farm) the mother and original of our Subject. Now all these by-places are so separated from each other by fields, meadows, hedge-rows, plantations, orchards, and the like, that they seem to be so many distinct little villages, uniting into one considerable town at the large street, in the middle of which stands the watch house. As I wish to see this last a more stately edifice ; so I long to have the whole space about it, from the new-Parade down to the Spread-eagle, neatly pitch'd : considering that flint stones are so near, so plentiful, and so cheap.

"Several persons, who have chosen this sweet place of Epsom for their constant abode, are distinguished from the rest by their habitations, as they are either by their birth or fortunes. As Sir John Ward's house on Clay Hill, Sir Edward Northey's‡ on Woodcote-green,

*Now South Street. †Probably the Hook Road of to-day. ‡Woodcote House.

and Mr. Rooth's in New-inn-lane,* whose canal on the top of a hill, with the soft walks on both sides, and the green mounts at each end, are very delightful. But among several other such houses, I shall make particular mention of only two. The first of these is Durdans, twice already mention'd ; tho' the place is so well known, that I need not say any thing to set off the grove, or the house, or the situation. But it were to be wished, that the right honourable the Lord Guilford, owner, would on the eminence (which bounds his noble avenue from the downs) erect a stone Pillar inscrib'd to Health and Liberty, as the air is the most pure in that place, and unconfin'd that can be. . . .

" The other house in Epsom that requires a special mention, is Mount Diston,† so nam'd from the owner, and from the round hillock near adjoining, which, rising gently on all sides in a conic figure, terminates on the summet in a circle which is a hundred foot diameter, and divided into four equal quarters. . . .

" But remembering, Madam, that I am to describe a village, and not a single house, I must needs say, that even the houses of the very townsmen are every where mighty neat, built most of 'em after the newest manner, and extremely convenient, being purposely contrived for the entertainment of strangers, and therefore beautify'd by the owners to the utmost of their ability, to which the ruins of Nonsuch-palace have not a little contributed. The fronts are adorn'd throughout with rows of elms or lime-trees, in many places artificially wreathed into verdant Porticos, cut into variety of figures, and close enough wrought to defend those, who sit under such hospitable shades, from the injuries of the sun and the rain. Here sometimes breakfast and supper are taken, as at other times a cheerful glass and a pipe ; for these vegetable canopies, in the very heat of the day, yield a grateful and refreshing coolness by the fanning breezes they collect from the delicate air of the downs. The finest of 'em all is that which shades the pav'd terrass in the centre of the town, extended quite along before the chief tavern and coffee

*The Elms, often called the "Clock House." †Woodcote Grove.

house. By the conversation of those that walk there,
you would fancy yourself to be this minute on the
Exchange, and the next minute at St. James's ; one
while in an East-India factory or a West-India planta-
tion, and another while with the army in Flanders or
on board the fleet in the ocean. Nor is there any
profession, trade, or calling, that you can miss of here,
either for your instruction or for your diversion. Fronting
this our Forum (as I may well call it) there is another
of these shades, lately wrought over a pav'd walk of
considerable length, which I just now called the New
Parade. Behind the houses are handsome tho' not
large Gardens, generally furnish'd with pretty walks,
and planted with variety of salads and fruit trees ;
which in several of 'em are all left free for the lodgers.
. . . Thus when you are on the top of the downs, 'tis
one of the lovliest prospects imaginable, to view in
the vale below such an agreeable mixture of trees and
buildings, that a stranger is at a loss to know (as it has
been observ'd of my beloved city Leyden in Holland)
whether it be a town in a wood or a wood in a town. . .

  " The two rival Bowling-greens are not to be forgot,
on which all the company by turns after diverting
themselves in the morning according to their different
fancies, make a gallant appearance every evening
(especially on Saturdays and Mondays) musick playing
most of the day, and dancing sometimes crowning the
night : as every new comer is awaken'd out of his sleep
the first morning, by the same music, which goes to
welcome them to Epsom. The Ladies, to show their
innate inclination to variety, are constantly tripping
from one green to the other ; and the Men are not more
sure to follow 'em, than glad of the occasion, to excuse
their own no less propensity to change. . . . In the
raffling shops are lost more hearts than guineas, tho'
Cupid be no where so liberal as in England. And the
greatest order, that in such cases can be expected
(however to me it be a rout) is preserv'd at the gaming
tables of every kind ; where it is very diverting for a
stander by to observe the different humors and passions
of both sexes, which discover themselves with less art

and reserve at play, than on any other occasion. There
you'll see a sparkish young fellow of twenty-five, sitting
right over a blooming beauty of eighteen, but so intent
on gain and the dice that he never exchanges a word
or a look with her. . . .

" The Taverns, the Inns and the Coffee-houses answer
the resort of the place. And I must do our Coffee-
houses the justice to affirm, that for social virtue they
are equal'd by few, and exceeded by none, tho' I wish
they may be imitated by all. A Tory does not stare
and leer when a Whig comes in, nor a Whig look sour
and whisper at the sight of a Tory. These distinctions
are laid by with the winter suit at London, and a gayer
easier habit worn in the country : even foreigners have
no reason to complain of being ill receiv'd in this part
of the Island. . . . as England is the plentifullest
country on earth, so no part of it is supply'd with more
diversity of the best provisions, both from within itself
and from adjacent villages, than Epsom. The nearness
of London does in like manner afford it all the exotic
preparatives and allurements to luxury, whenever any
is disposed to make a sumptuous banquet, or to give
a genteel collation. You wou'd think yourself in some
enchanted camp to see the peasants ride to every house
with the choicest fruits, herbs, roots, and flowers, with
all sorts of tame and wild fowl, with the rarest fish and
venison, and with every kind of butcher's meat, among
which Banstead-down mutton is the most relishing dainty.

" Thus to see the fresh and artless damsels of the
plain, either accompany'd by their amorous swains or
aged parents, striking their bargains with the wise
court and city Ladies, who, like Queens in a Tragedy,
display all their finery on benches before their doors
(where they hourly censure and are censur'd) and to
observe, how the handsomest of each degree equally
admire, envy, and cozen one another, is to me one of
the chief amusements of the place. . . . Even Venus
had a mole ; and gossipping is the greatest objection
I have ever heard made to Epsom. . . .

" The old Wells at half a mile's distance, which
formerly us'd to be the meeting place in the forenoon,

A SEMI-BIRD'S-EYE VIEW OF EPSOM AS IT PROBABLY APPEARED ABOUT 1700.

The houses are chiefly named according to Toland's description.

are not at present so much in vogue ; the waters, they say, being found as good within the village, and all diversions in greater perfection. The view from the fertile Common in which they lye, is, as from every elevation hereabouts, wonderfully delightful ; especially so distinct a prospect of London at so great a distance. But the fortuitous cure of a leprous shepherd (an origin attributed to these in common with other such Wells) appears even hence to be fabulous, that they have never since had the like effect : tho' otherwise these aluminous waters are experienc'd to be very beneficial in gently cleansing the body, in cooling the head, and purifying the blood ; the salt, that is chymically made of 'em, being famous over all Europe. . . . The hunting of a Pig there every monday morning, when the only knack consists in catching and holding him up by the tail, is infinitely more becoming the boys that perform it, than the spectators that employ 'em. . . .

"But to shift our scenes from the ring on the most eminent part of the Downs, where I have often counted above sixty coaches on a Sunday evening, and whence the painter must take his view when he represents Epsom, you may distinctly see nine or ten counties in whole or in part. Besides the imperial city of London, very many considerable towns, and an infinite number of country seats, you also see the two Royal Palaces of Windsor and Hampton-Court. Within a mile and a half is the place, and only the place, where the other splendid Palace of Nonsuch lately stood (Footnote by Toland—a great part of it stood in my own time, and I have spoken with those that saw it entire). . . .

"In two or three hours time I can be at London, when ever I will, at my ease ; and, if I have no business in town, I can receive all the public news as well, and almost as soon, at Epsom : several stage coaches going and returning every day, with town and Country wag-gons more than once a week; not to mention the ordinary post that arrives every morning Sundays excepted."

With the aid of this wonderfully graphic account and other information, I have been enabled to produce a semi-birdseye view of Epsom in 1700. I do not suggest that it is accurate in every detail, but from old prints and from the houses of two hundred years ago still standing, a very near approach to actuality is possible.

In the centre of the High Street was the little plaster walled Watch House with its quaint clock turret at one end, and adjoining it was the pond spoken of elsewhere. The two rival bowling greens seem also to have been in the centre of the street. Along the front of the houses were the rows of limes and elms, and bushes clipped into all sorts of quaint shapes. The houses themselves, with the exception of the New Inn and the other smaller hostelries, were chiefly low and unpretentious—one may see them to-day in the row opposite Waterloo House. With the clipped trees, the tiled roofs, the cream coloured and red brick walls as a background, one must add a foreground of contemporary figures— the men in great white powdered wigs, elaborate coats of plum-coloured velvet or of any other colour or material, sleeves with long lace at the wrists, knee breeches, silk stockings, and square toed, large buckled shoes. So elaborate was the dress of the Court ladies of this period that I cannot do better than quote Leigh Hunt's "Memoirs of Sir Ralph Esher." "The dress at that time was well calculated to set off a woman to advantage. Lady Castlemaine was dressed in white and green, with an open boddice of pink looped in diamonds. Her sleeves were green, looped up full to the shoulders with jewelry, and showing the white shift beneath, richly trimmed with lace. The boddice was long and close with a very low tucker. The petticoat fell in ample folds, but not so long as to keep the ankle unexposed ; and it was relieved from an appearance of too much weight by the very weightiness of the hanging sleeves, which counterpoising its magnitude, and looking flowery with lace and ribbons, left the arms free at the elbows and fell down behind on either side. The hair was dressed wide with ringlets at the cheeks ; and the fair vision held a fan in one hand, while the Duke led her by the other."

The High Street in 1660.

There were numbers of sedan chairs and coaches, and servants and post-boys innumerable.

The depraved state of the morals of this period is reflected in various publications still in existence ; one of them, entitled "Merry Newes from Epsom Wells," is so revolting that it seems inconceivable that it should have ever been published.

At last there appeared one Levingstone, an apothecary who set up as a doctor in Epsom, and by the year of Queen Anne's accession, had made a considerable fortune out of the wealthy visitors. This rascally fellow conceived the idea of starting a new well, which, with more sumptuous buildings and still greater entertainments would attract the folk from the old well to his own. He succeeded as only crafty and unscrupulous men can, ingratiating himself meanwhile by presenting a piece of land in East Street (where the present almshouses now stand) for the erection of an almshouse for twelve widows. In 1706 he purchased some land in the town from Sir John Parsons, and, says Brayley, "built a large house, with an assembly room for dancing and music, and other apartments, for raffling, hazard, and probably all sorts of gambling ; together with shops for milliners, jewellers, toymen, and other trades people who dealt chiefly in fashionable luxuries. He planted a grove and laid out a bowling green, at the end of which he sunk a well with a pump adapted to it, and by means of subterraneous pipes, conveyed the water into a basin at the extremity of the assembly room. The arrangements were completed in about two years ; and at this place, to which the proprietor gave the name of the *New Wells,* he gave concerts and balls, set up gaming tables, and by the novelty of his entertainments, he drew the company from the old wells." From this description one would be led to believe that Levingstone's new well house was "Waterloo House" of to-day, but this can scarcely be so for it is spoken of at this time as an inn. "The New Wells" must have been pulled down or the building was converted into a private house, for what eventually

Levingstone the Apothecary.

became of the place is quite forgotten. A certain percentage of those who were induced to forsake the old well really came to drink the waters, and these soon discovered that there was no efficacy in the water from the new wells. Here was a danger our apothecary might well be alarmed at. But luck being as usual with him, in 1715 he found a means of preventing these odious comparisons between his spurious and the real mineral waters. In that year a lease of the old wells was granted or renewed to John Grant, John Maynard, and Daniel Ellicar, and being by this time a wealthy man, the apothecary seems to have purchased or in some way obtained an assignment of the lease to himself. He at once locked up the honest well and by this means forced everyone to drink the water at the new well, which was as little able to purify the blood as that of Woodcote Pond.

All this deception brought Epsom wells into disfavour.
The decline Tunbridge Wells began to flourish, and
of Epsom our speculating apothecary correspondingly
as a noticed year by year the steady falling off
Watering at Epsom. This doubtless hastened his
Place. death, for in 1727 Levingstone died.

When Queen Anne held her court at Windsor, her Consort, Prince George of Denmark, was in the habit of visiting Epsom to drink the waters, and his presence helped to attract many who came for health or dissipation. During the boom in trade followed by the South Sea Company, the town was immensely popular, but at the bursting of the Bubble in 1720 Epsom began to be deserted.

The old well was reopened about 1727, considerable repairs were made to the old rooms there, and it was once more patronised as a medicinal spring.

But it was not much frequented by strangers, being more the resort of the local gentry who organised public breakfasts there every Monday in the summer. After a time this also was dropped. Yet another gleam of publicity flickered at Epsom in connection with Mrs. Mapp, the extraordinary bone setter. Frantic efforts were made to induce her to stop in the town, but after her marriage she moved to London, and left Epsom to its fate.

Yet another blow came when in 1753 Dr. Richard Russel introduced sea bathing. The diversion in this direction was absolutely fatal to Epsom. The very

SOME OF THE REMAINING TREES IN THE DORKING ROAD.
They formed a portion of the avenue leading from the Town to the Wells
on Epsom Common.

last attempt to revive interest in the Epsom wells, was between 1760 and 1770, when a Dr. Dale Ingram advertised a preparation of magnesia, obtained from the mineral waters, and opened the rooms for public breakfasts. No success attended this scheme, and the buildings gradually fell into complete dilapidation. In 1804 the regrettable demolition of the well house took place, and a Mr. Hichener, who had either purchased or taken on lease the ground where the well stood, built a small house for himself there, leaving the well and the old wall enclosing the garden intact.

To-day the well is shaded by fruit trees near the tennis lawn of the garden surrounding the modern house now called "The Wells." One piece of the original brickwork of the old structures round the well has been incorporated into the back wall of a green-house, but beyond this there is nothing of interest to be seen. The waters themselves still retain their original qualities.

The Wells to-day.

George III and his Queen paid a visit to Epsom in 1767. A cutting from a contemporary publication says: "The King and Queen came to Epsom immediately after the nomination (of two members) in an open chaise, attended with only three outriders, made a very short stay, and returned afterwards to Richmond to dinner."

Traces of another feature of Epsom in the days of its fame are to be seen in the rows of elms and limes still scattered about the town and approaches to the wells. From near Hylands House to the commencement of the common, there is quite a fine avenue of these trees. As one approaches Stamford Green from West Hill, there are nine pollard elms in a row on the left-hand side of the road, while in the gardens in front of the cottages by the "Marquis of Granby" Inn, there are some very knarled and closely trimmed specimens. Others are by the "Magpie" in South Street, in a little front garden nearly opposite the "King's Head," in front of one of the very old houses in Church Street, at the corner of Woodcote Green, and shading a quaint house near the alms-houses in East Street.

Many of the scenes of the late Sir Walter Besant's "Chaplain of the Fleet" are laid at Epsom, the author mentioning a number of the old features of the place, the story being woven into the period of its declining

popularity.   There is one description which shows a
limited knowledge of the topography of Epsom ; the
passage runs, " I left the house (Woodcote End House)
and walked up the hill, intending to find the three gentlemen waiting for their duel.   These meetings generally
took place, I knew, on the way to the old well. I left Durdans on the right, and struck across the turf to the left."
Leaving Durdans on the right would take one across
fields in the direction of the Burgh Heath Road, and if
left were intended, Durdans is so situated that it would
be too far to the left to be used in a description of a
walk towards the old well, right away on the further
side of the Common.

THE WELL AS IT APPEARS TO-DAY.

CHAPTER IV.

IN WHICH AN ACCOUNT IS GIVEN OF
THE CHURCHES OF EPSOM.

THE churches of Epsom do not possess many features of antiquarian interest, the Parish Church, dedicated to St. Martin, having been rebuilt, with the exception of the tower, in 1824, and Christ Church on Epsom Common being an entirely modern building.

St. Martin's stands on slightly rising ground, on the east side of Church Street, with Pit Place on the south, and a brewery, fortunately of a very inoffensive external appearance, between the graveyard and the road. A short turning, useful both to the brewery and the church, leads one to a series of wide flagged steps, running along the west front.

The Parish Church.

The building is, to quote a quaint guide published in 1825, "a handsome Gothic structure . . . at once simple and elegant," and in the words of a more recent writer, "a new pseudo-Gothic structure of the commonest type." A glance at the church is sufficient to prove the correctness of the second opinion. The walls are built of brick with a facing of broken flints and dressings of white stone. The blue slate roof, the insufficient wooden mullions of the windows, the painted doors and painted interior woodwork, all tend to impress the idea of a cheap imitation of Gothic, but there is nothing extraordinary in this, for at this period buildings of the same type were multiplying on the face of the country with ·such rapidity under the admiring gaze of the general public.

EPSOM PARISH CHURCH, DEDICATED TO ST. MARTIN.

The stone lion on the right belongs to Pit Place, and is believed to have come from Nonsuch Palace.

E

In the tower there is a welcome look of solidity. It is flint-faced like the rest of the building, with an octagonal turret at the north-west corner, while above rises a very sharp and slender little shingled spire, terminating in a cross and weather vane. This is the oldest portion of the building, for when the old church was being pulled down, it was found that the tower was quite strong enough to remain. It contains a clock and eight bells, some of which have quaint inscriptions, with dates about 1730. Inside the church the light is much diminished by galleries in both aisles. The walls are coloured with a pale brown distemper and the panelled fronts of the galleries are also painted a brownish colour.

But despite these features, there is an indescribable air of late Georgian quaintness about the church, and with the added interest of the many seventeenth century monuments saved from the former building, there are few who would fail to find some charm about the place.

With the exception of the east window of the chancel, all are filled with plain leaded glass. The east window, designed and constructed by Mr. F. A. Oldaker, of Epsom, was unveiled at Christmas, 1892. In the centre is our Lord as the "Light of the world," with representations of St. Gabriel and St. Raphael on either side. At the time of the opening of the church, the window was filled with stained glass executed by Willement, a heraldic painter to George IV. The central light contained a whole length figure of the Saviour copied from Leonardo da Vinci. Those who are curious to see the details of this window will find a coloured engraving of it in Pownall's History of Epsom, of which a few copies exist. Mr. Hatchard, the architect of the new church, was at great pains to preserve the features of the old building, the curve of the arches and the mouldings of the columns being exact replicas of the former ones. The area of the church is slightly larger than the old one, the west front having been advanced seven feet and the side walls three feet beyond the former limits. Through the lengthening of the aisles, the chancel has been shortened

considerably, and is not separated from the nave
architecturally. The roof is of a very low pitch; it is
coloured with a pale blue distemper, and supported by
trusses forming flat arches which support the main
rafters. Pillars of Portland stone, consisting of four
slender columns surrounding a central shaft, support
the five arches on either side of the nave.

Under the tower is the font, described by Brayley as
ancient, although the precise date of it is uncertain.
It is entirely octagonal, with the upper portion decorated
with quatrefoil panels, Tudor roses, a well carved fish
and sundry heads and shields. Formerly the pulpit
was of painted wood, "in imitation of wainscot," but
this has made way for one of honest oak.

THE CARVED SPANISH MAHOGANY CHEST IN THE VESTRY OF
ST. MARTIN'S CHURCH, EPSOM.

The organ occupies the north transept, and where
the south transept should be there is a vestry containing

perhaps the most interesting object in the whole structure—an Elizabethan Spanish mahogany chest. It stands nearly four feet high, and its sides are entirely covered with delicately carved and inlaid figures in Elizabethan costume. I have been unable to find any written record of this chest.

On the south wall of the chancel are nine monuments, most of them of white marble on a grey **The Monuments.** marble background. The highest and most easterly one is by Flaxman. A whole length female figure is shown with her head reclining in grief on a votive urn, to the memory of John Henry Warre (of the ancient family of Warre of Westercombe, in Somerset), also to Mrs. Braithwaite Warre, his widow, who died in 1824.

Adjoining is an urn supported by two whole length female figures. It is to the memory of Mrs. Jane Rowe, daughter of Hutton Rowe, Esq., of Haswell Moor, Durham. The last monument on this line shows a bust of the Rev. Jonathan Boucher, M.A., resting upon a sarcophagus. He was for nineteen years vicar of this parish and died in 1804.

Commencing again at the east, another of Flaxman's creations shows another figure with her arm resting on an urn which stands upon a pillar. The inscription is a eulogy recalling the virtues of John Braithwaite, Esq., who was born in the Island of Barbadoes. He served the island in a public character and at his death in 1800, at the age of seventy-eight, seems to have been very much respected.

The adjoining tablet has a figure of Hope with an anchor on one side, and on the other a woman whose head is shrouded in a hood, also by Flaxman. This is to the Rev. John Parkhurst, M.A., of Epsom, a descendant of the Parkhursts of Catesby, in Northamptonshire. The inscription further states that he was distinguished "by deep and laborious researches into the treasures of Divine learning; the fruits of which are preserved in two valuable Lexicons." In the graveyard just by the east side of the vestry is a table-shaped tomb of red brick, and on the flat stone

top another Parkhurst is made famous in the often
quoted lines :

Here Lyeth the Carcase
Of Honest CHARLES PARKHURST,
Who nere could Dance or Sing,
But allways was True to
His Sovereign Lord the King,
CHARLES THE FIRST.
Ob. Dec. xx.   MDCCIV.
Etat LXXXVI.

Next to the Parkhurst monument is one by Chantrey.
It shows a woman kneeling with an infant in her arms,
and is in memory of Susan, wife of John Ashley Warre,
Esq., who died in 1820, and was followed a few months
later by her infant son, John Braithwaite Warre.

Commencing once more from the east, the first tablet
is to the memory of Peak Garland, Esq., born at Epsom
in 1778, and died in 1841. The Garland family, it will
be remembered, gave their name to the house now
known as Woodcote Grove, the residence of Mr. A. W.
Aston. The two remaining tablets in the chancel are
to Mary Ashley, who died in 1845, and Benjamin Pugh.

Under the gallery on the east wall of the south aisle,
one may notice two very chaste-looking monuments
with the inscriptions surrounded by circular wreaths.
The one to the north, by Flaxman, to Miss Eleanor
Belfield, daughter of the Rev. Finney Belfield, of
Primley Hall, Devon, who died in 1802 at the age of
fifteen, has within the circle a sculptured lily severed
from its stem. In the other circle appears the name
of Rebecca, wife of Rev. John Gibbons, and niece of
John Braithwaite, who died in 1815. The next
monument is to the memory of William Haygarth, A.M.,
who was "deeply skilled in the learning and antiquities
of Greece and Italy." On the other side of the vestry
door is a white marble slab with a very long inscription
recording the benefactions of Elizabeth Culling.

A short distance from this, on the south wall, is a
most interesting memorial. The inscription
is in Latin and surrounded by massive
columns and a pediment. It is in memory
of Richard Evelyn of Woodcote, brother
to John Evelyn, the diarist, of Wotton,

The
Monument
to Richard
Evelyn.

near Leith Hill. Richard Evelyn died in 1669—his wife Elizabeth twenty-two years later. Her monument, a very elaborate marble one of similar construction to that of her husband erected by Charles Calvert, Lord Baltimore, may be seen on the staircase to the south gallery. On the south wall there are other monuments to the Cuthbert family of Woodcote (it is spelt Woodcott in the inscription), to Francis Vernon Northey, who died fighting in Zululand, to John Pierce, and to the Bury and James families.

On the floor of the south aisle just beneath Richard Evelyn's monument is a small and scarcely legible brass. It says:

"Hic jacet Willm' Marston Armig q'obiit
Vo die january Ao. Mo. Dc. XI CIII' me' de mi' . . ."

This seems to refer to William Merston, who was lord of the manor of Horton which then included Woodcote Park. The date of his death, 1511, agrees with Brayley's statement.

Upon the wall of the south gallery are monuments to John Lloyd, who died in 1718, and Edward Knipe of Hookfield Grove (now the residence of Mr. Basil Braithwaite). The north gallery has monuments to Elizabeth Price, who died in 1825; the Rev. Owen Ludgater, a minister of the parish, who died in 1703 at the early age of thirty-one; and the family monument of the Trotter family of Horton Manor. Included in the names recorded hereon is that of Elizabeth Trotter, the founder of Christ Church on Epsom Common. Under the north gallery on a small black marble tablet, bearing the arms of Coke and Berkeley, is a long Latin inscription to Robert Coke, who died in 1643. Brayley states that beneath this was a white fronted altar tomb with a black marble slab on the top, but this has been removed. Further to the east on this wall, in a very ornate marble border, is an inscription running, "Here lyeth ye body of Robert Coke, late of Nonsuch, Esq., youngest son of Clement Coke ye 6th son of ye Rt. Honble. Sir Edward Coke, late Ld. Chief Justice of England. He married Theophila, youngest daughter of Arthur Coke, Esq., by Elizabeth, sole heiress of Sir George Waldegrave, of Hitch-ham, in Suffolk, Kt., he left issue one son and one daughter. After he had faithfully served as a commander his late Majesty, King Charles ye 1st, and lived to see ye disappointment of his enemies in ye restauration and above 20 years reign of our present sovereign, peaceably departed this life at Nonsuch, ye 23rd day of June in ye 59th year of his age in ye year of our Lord 1681."

An interesting glimpse of a congregation on Sunday, in 1667, may be gained from Pepys's Diary on that date :—"July 14th, 1667. Mr. Evelyn with his lady, and also my Lord George Barkeley's lady, and their fine daughter, that the King of France liked so well, and did dance so rich in jewells before the King at the ball I was at at Oak Court last winter, and also their son, a Knight of the Bath, were at church this morning."

Over the centre doorway of the nave and under the west gallery are the royal arms, while on the wall of the west end may be seen inscribed the many charities left for the benefit of the poor. They are too numerous to mention in detail, but are chiefly for teaching poor children, clothing old men and women, and supplying food and fuel (in the will of Mrs. Mary Dundas it is spoken of as sea coal) to needy but honest folk.

The graveyard possesses a large number of richly

The Churchyard. carved eighteenth century tombstones, where scythes, hourglasses, skulls, and cherubs' heads all have their place. All the best of this type are on the south or south-east parts of the churchyard, and one is particularly noticeable on account of its having the front surface rounded. Quite a number of these stones record the trade of the man who has passed away, masons, painters, plumbers, and tinworkers being among the number. Near the centre of the east portion of the graveyard is the family tomb of the Northey family of Woodcote. The inscription, a long one running round the sides, is in Latin, and is barely decipherable. The first name is that of Sir Edward Northey, Attorney-General in the reigns of William III, Anne, and George I. Very quaint indeed are the lines on a tomb near the tower.

CHRIST CHURCH, EPSOM COMMON.

From the Pond on Stamford Green.

They are to Julia, Eliza, Edwin, and Julia *(sic)* Langlands, but there is no date.

> Here also lie four pretty buds
> Lately made of flesh and blood,
> The cup of life, just with their lips they pressed,
> Found the taste bitter, and declined the rest.
> Averse—then turning from the face of day
> They softly sighed their little souls away.

In the thirteenth century, the living of Epsom as well

Early History of the Church.
as the manor, belonged to the Abbot of
Chertsey, who had a moiety of the tithes
before it was appropriated. In a rental of
the manor of Ebbisham, taken in the
eleventh year of King Henry VII, 1496,
when Thomas Piggott was Abbot of Chertsey, it is
interesting to know that it is stated that " Alice Hyde
holds a cottage lately built on the lord's waste near
Stamford Chapel." All traces of the chapel have disappeared, and it was probably on its decay or suppression
that John Merston, Esq., in 1453, obtained a licence for
building a chantry in Epsom Church. In 1538, the
rectory was purchased from the Abbey, with the manor,
by Henry VIII, and the same year was granted there-
with to Sir Nicholas Carew. After the attainder of this
new owner, the rectory and manor remained with the
Crown until the 31st year of Elizabeth's reign, when
they were granted by the Queen to Edward D'Arcy. It
would not be kind to ask the reader to flounder through
the successive changes of ownership of rectory and
manor down to the present day, but those who wish to
have every detail will find a complete list of Patrons
and Rectors in Manning and Bray's History of Surrey.

Rising sedately from the furze and bracken of Epsom

Christ Church.
Common is Christ Church. So solid and
simple is the square tower with its south-
west corner turret, and so suggestive of the
typical English country church is the combination of
red tiled roof with white flint and stonework, that from
a short distance a stranger would not pronounce it
modern. The church was founded in 1843 as a chapel
of ease to St. Martin's chiefly by Elizabeth Trotter,
daughter of Mr. James Trotter of Horton Manor who

on making a bequest of £8,000 stipulated that there should be no "Ritualistic nonsense" in connection with the new church. It was originally intended as a convenience for the poorer inhabitants of Epsom Common, the walk to the Parish Church being a fairly long one. The first building was of red brick, holding about two hundred people, and was considered to be a rather pretty structure. Mr. J. Ivatt Briscoe, the lord of the manor, gave the site, while contributions to the building fund were made by Her Majesty the Queen-Dowager, the Bishop of Winchester, the Earl of Egmont, Sir Gilbert Heathcote, Mr. W. J. Davison, and Mr. John Trotter. Besides these a sum of £300 was granted by the Church Building and the Diocesan Church Building Societies. In 1874 the little brick structure became too small for the congregation, and the present church, designed by Sir A. Blomfield, was erected and consecrated by the Bishop of Winchester in 1876. The south aisle was added later by Lord Rosebery, and the tower was only finished as recently as 1889, the bells being hung in the following year, and the beautiful clock with chimes not long after.

Before the completion of the present church, the *London Gazette* of July 10, 1874, published the order in council delimiting the boundaries of the "New Parish of Christ Church, Epsom Common," and from that day forth the building was a chapel of ease no longer.

The Institution of the Parish.

The style of the church is decorated Gothic, and although the interior of the chancel and north transept is now very richly ornamented, the nave and aisles are simple almost to severity. The aisles are separated from the nave by arcades of four pointed arches supported by pillars consisting of four clustered around a central shaft. The spandrels of the arches are ornamented with small but beautifully carved angels' heads. Four sets of lancet windows light each aisle. They have been gradually filled with very good stained glass and now present a series of pictures, in proper sequence, of the life of our Lord. The central space of the three-light window at the west end of the south aisle is filled with a stained glass representation of a Grecian soldier resting on his spear. It is a very beautiful piece of work, and fittingly preserves the memory of Francis Vernon Northey, Lieut.-Col. of the 60th Rifles, who died from a mortal wound received at the battle of Ginghilova, in Zululand, on Palm Sunday, 6th April, 1879. The marble memorial to Lieut.-Col. Northey in the south wall of St. Martin's church has already been mentioned. In the south transept is the organ—its fine quality, together with the ability of the organist and choir, having made the music at Christ Church a synonym for excellence throughout the neighbourhood. The two side panels and the painting on the organ are to the memory of Leonard John Hunter, the younger son of the vicar, the Rev. Canon Archer G. Hunter. Close to the organ a brass is inserted in the wall—the inscription runs, "The east window of this chancel is offered in grateful remembrance of Elizabeth Trotter, who, by the Grace of God, was founder of this church and parish. She was the daughter of James Trotter, Esq., of Horton Manor, and died Oct. 25, A.D. 1868." The glass of the window is very beautiful indeed, although the wheel pattern tracery does not give so stately an appearance as perpendicular work.

Two shining brasses in the north transept proclaim that the very elaborate and many-coloured mosaic work round the east window was completed in 1887, and that it was placed there to the memory of William Trotter of Horton Manor, also that the marble reredos was erected in 1886, in memory of Mrs. Mary Elizabeth Trotter, who died in 1885. The red and white encaustic tiles—known to the makers, at least, as opus sectile—which occupy the lower portion of the walls of the chancel, were placed there in December, 1900, to the memory of Norman Withall Aston, who died at Eton College at the age of seventeen. At the same time as the tiles were being inserted, the whole of the remaining untreated portion of the walls of the chancel were covered with decorative frescoes—the

The Decoration of the Chancel.

paint being relieved with gilding, while the roof is now
of a slate green tone without the interference of any
other colour. It was a difficult and daring piece of
work to place so much ornament in so small a space,
but the designers (Powell, of Whitefriars) may be said
to have met with a fair measure of success. The three-
light window in the north transept is to the memory of
Charles Vernon Strange, a lieutenant in the Royal Navy
and lord of the manor of Epsom, who was lost in the
H.M.S. "Eurydice" off the Isle of Wight on March 24th,
1878. In the narthex at the west end of the nave, one may
see six little quatrefoil windows, filled with stained glass,
to the memory of the three infant children of William
and Mary Elizabeth Trotter. Both the font and pulpit
are of richly carved white stone, while the roof is of
open timber, and when it has gathered to itself the
dignity of years will probably, with the rest of the
building, be considered an architectural treasure. The
churchyard is nicely kept and includes a fir coppice, and
a useful little shed for storing the bicycles of those who
come to the services from a considerable distance.

In connection with Christ Church there is, in the
Hook Road, a little corrugated iron church,

St.
Barnabas's,
Hook Road.

dedicated to St. Barnabas. Christchurch
Room, standing on a piece of ground in
West Hill presented by Mr. G. H. Longman,
a very well built little hall, was opened by Lord
Rosebery in 1899.

The interesting old Congregational Chapel in Church
Street stands back from the road behind

The
Congregational
Chapel.

its well-kept graveyard in a very retiring
fashion, and one might easily pass without
noticing it. In the latter years of the
eighteenth century, Dr. Isaac Watts, the hymn writer,
used to occasionally preach there when stopping with
Sir John Hartopp, Bart. The house, it is stated, nearly
adjoined the chapel, and is believed to be the charming
old building known now as "The Acacias," facing the
end of the Worple Road. After this period the chapel
fell into a sad state of dilapidation, and was in 1803
used as a barn; indeed, so ruinous was its condition

that the heavens could be seen through the roof. Large square pews remained at the sides of the building, but the central portion was filled with agricultural implements. Tattered curtains and mouldering hymn books completed the dismal condition of the place.

It was a Mr. Atkinson, a friend of the owner of the chapel, who set to work to repair the building at a cost of nearly £500, which was made up in part by subscriptions. In 1819 the freehold of the place came into the hands of a personage whose doctrines were considered very objectionable, and until 1824 the church languished. Somewhere about this time there came a minister, Dr. John Harris, whose preaching before long rendered him quite famous, so that the chapel was frequently crowded. Even the gentry were wont to put in an appearance, and there was so little accommodation for every one that the steps to the gallery had to be requisitioned as additional seats. It is as author of "Mammon," a book which had an immense sale, that Dr. Harris will perhaps be remembered, although he was Chairman of the Congregational Union of England and Wales in 1852. To-day the chapel bears the date 1846 very prominently on the gable end—the year of the last restoration. The quaintest feature still to be seen is a little square opening in the partition of the porch through which the coffin was thrust during the burial service. It is much to be hoped that no spirit of improvement will lead to the removal of this odd little survival.

CHAPTER V.

A DESCRIPTION

OF WOODCOTE, DURDANS, AND SOME

OTHER GREAT HOUSES.

BETWEEN the town itself and the Downs lies that portion of Epsom known as Woodcote—considered as a separate place in the seventeenth century and even now divided from the town by meadows. It is one of those rare spots where one finds a number of seventeenth century houses and mansions with their grounds adjoining one another, so that nothing modern or cheap has been allowed to intrude, Woodcote bearing much the same appearance to-day as it did in 1680. The timber, if magnificent then, is magnificent to-day, the birds, doubtless reduced in numbers, are still well represented, the lanes are still quiet and reposeful, and the houses, in most cases altered and added to, are conspicuous by their appearance of well preserved antiquity.

Woodcote Green, with the road on one side rising up to the Common between high banks and great overhanging elms, has on its south side Woodcote House, the seat of the Northeys since the time of Queen Anne and now in the possession of the Rev. Edward William Northey, lord of the manors of Cheam, Ewell, and Cuddington. The first reference to the house in old writings is by Toland, in 1711, who refers to "Sir Edward Northey's on Woodcote Green." This Sir Edward Northey was Attorney General in the reigns of Anne, William III,

Woodcote House.

and George I, and was the descendant of John Northey, who had lands at Bradwell, in Essex, in the year 1511. There is an oft quoted story concerning Sir Edward on which doubt has been thrown, although there is every possibility of its being true. It states that the first brood of rooks forming the origin of the historic rookery existing in King's Bench Walk in the Temple up till about 1800, was brought from Woodcote by Sir Edward Northey during the reign of Queen Anne.

SIR EDWARD NORTHEY,

Attorney General in the Reigns of Anne, William III, and George I.
From a Photograph of the Painting at Woodcote House.

Of the original Woodcote House only a portion remains, the greater part of the building being of a later date—the roofs being slated and the walls covered with stucco. In the dining room hang paintings of Sir Edward Northey and his successors and also a portrait of Queen Anne by Lely. Although surrounded by plenty of trees, the views from the house across the sweeping green valley towards Woodcote Park are very lovely.

Mr. E. R. Northey, J.P., father of the present
Mr. Northey, died in December, 1878, at the age of
eighty-four. He entered the 52nd Light Infantry at
the age of 16, and served with that regiment in the
Peninsular War in 1813. After recovering from a
wound received at Vittoria, Mr. Northey was present
at Waterloo. After settling down at Epsom he was
Deputy-Lieutenant, and was in 1856 High Sheriff of
Surrey.

The entrance to Woodcote Park is opposite Baron's
Pond on Epsom Common, scarcely half-a-

Woodcote   mile from Woodcote Green. So surrounded
Park.   by its splendid trees is the mansion that
even in winter scarcely a glimpse of it may be seen outside the limits of the park. Richard Evelyn, brother of
John Evelyn, the diarist of Wotton, according to
Brayley, was struck with the situation of Woodcote
Park, and there seems little doubt that the mansion he
built was constructed on the site of the monastic
building which at one time stood there, the decorative
work by Grinling Gibbons and Verrio being carried
out at this time at the suggestion of John Evelyn.

Horton manor, including Woodcote Park, formerly
belonged, with the manor of Epsom, to the Abbots of
Chertsey, but in the reign of Henry VI the Abbot
granted Horton to John Merston and Rose his wife.
In 1511 William Merston died, leaving his two
daughters Joan and Ursula his co-heirs. Ursula married
a Nicholas Myn, one of whose descendants sold the
estate to George Mynn, Esq. His only son having
died without issue, the Horton property came into the
possession of Elizabeth, the elder daughter

Richard   of George Mynn, who married Richard
Evelyn.   Evelyn on the 16th of August, 1648. John
Evelyn refers to the wedding in his diary under that
date. " I went to Woodcote to the wedding of my
brother Richard, who married the daughter and coheire
of Esquire Minn, lately deceas'd, by which he had a
greate estate, both in land and monie, on the death of
a brother. The coach in which the bride and the
bridegroome were, was overturn'd in coming home, but

no harm was done them." In 1655 John Evelyn states
that he spent "the rest of Christmas at my brother's,
R. Evelyn at Woodcot," and from March 3rd to the
21st, 1670, there are references to the illness and death
(on the 7th) of Richard at his "noble seate at Woodcote
neere Epsom." On March 21st the entry runs, "we all
accompanied the corpse of my dear brother to Epsom
Church, where he was decently interr'd in the chapell
belonging to Woodcote House.* A great number of
friends and gentlemen of the country attended, about
twenty coaches and six horses and innumerable people."

Elizabeth Evelyn, having survived her husband and
children, left the manor of Horton and Woodcote Park
to Charles Calvert, fourth Lord Baltimore, an Irish
peer, maternally descended from George Mynn of
Hertingfordbury, in Hertfordshire. The Baltimores
held the property until Frederick, the seventh lord, sold
it to a Mr. Monk and left England for the Continent,
after the disgraceful affair brought to light at the
Kingston Assizes in 1768. Mr. Monk sold the property
to a Mr. Nelson, who in 1777 sold it again to Mr.
Arthur Cuthbert. Soon after his death in 1788, the
Woodcote Park property, separated from that of
Horton, was purchased by Mr. Lewis Teissier, a
merchant of London, whose son succeeded to the
property as Baron de Teissier—the title being granted
to him by Louis the Eighteenth in 1819 as a lineal
descendant of Teissier, Baron de Marguerittes and
Marquis de Lagarne in Languedoc.

In 1855 Woodcote Park was bought from Baron de
Teissier by Mr. Robert Brooks, whose son, Mr. Herbert
Brooks, now holds the property. According to Brayley,
Charles, sixth Lord Baltimore, "was founder of the
present mansion of Woodcote Park," but although he
may have almost entirely rebuilt the place, the
"founder" was undoubtedly Richard Evelyn. The
front of the house, of stone and stuccoed brick, with
its double flight of steps leading to the entrance hall,
is very imposing, although the style of architecture is
not generally accepted as most adapted to an English

*This refers to Woodcote Park, and not to the seat of the Northeys.

landscape.   Facing the main entrance and partially encircled on both sides by curving arcades of stone is a circular lawn surrounding a fountain.   Above the southern arcade there is a wide lawn of that typical velvety perfection which Americans are just beginning to discover has never been equalled in their own country. The lawn is backed by dense masses of foliage, but there are openings giving a view up the valley towards the Downs.   The house faces this valley and the views from the windows are towards the opposite ridge crowned with plantations of innumerable trees—some splendid scotch firs standing out conspicuously from the rest.

The entrance hall of the house has coupled Corinthian columns supporting a frieze. The whole of this woodwork is now painted white.   In the large drawing room the ceilings are elaborately decorated—the portion nearest to the hall is by Verrio, and represents the "Sacrifice to Diana ; " the further portion by Zuccarelli is entitled "The Muses." The centre of the ceiling of the adjoining room, known as the library, is by Rubens.   From this room there is an entrance to the apartment at one time used as a chapel—the fourth Lord Baltimore having been a Roman Catholic.   This ceiling, also by Verrio, shows a scene at the Resurrection. The altar formerly in this room is now in Ashtead Church.   On the doors of the drawing room, the brass locks, bearing the coronet of Lord Baltimore, are of wonderfully delicate workmanship, while those in the room immediately on the left of the main entrance are of silver and are still more elaborate.   These silver locks are said to be the work of French refugees, a number of whom visited Woodcote Park at the time of the first Revolution. But this may or may not be true.   In a gallery on the first floor are a series of painted panels illustrating the old Greek story of Daphnis and Chloe.   They were designed in 1718 by Phillip, Duke of Orleans, Regent of France during the minority of Louis XV.

The present building known as Durdans, belonging
Durdans.   to the Earl of Rosebery, is not an ancient
one, although a succession of houses have
stood on approximately the same site since George,

thirteenth Lord Berkeley built himself a house from the
materials of Nonsuch Palace, at the time of its demolition by the Duchess of Cleveland between the years
1670 and 1673. But even this may not have been the
original " Durdans," for in Evelyn's Diary there is an
entry dated August 14th, 1658 : " We went to Durdans
to a challeng'd match at bowls for 10*l.* which we wonn,"
and again in 1662 on the 1st of September : " Being
invited by Ld. Berkeley, I went to Durdans, Epsom,
where dined his Majestie (Charles II), the Queene,
Duke, Dutchesse, Prince Rupert, Prince Edward, and
abundance of noblemen. I went after dinner to visit
my brother of Woodcot." On the same day Pepys
writes, September 1st : " With Sir W. Batten by coach
to St. James', this being the first day of our meeting
there by the Duke's order ; but when we come we
found him going out by coach with his Duchess, and
he told us he was to go abroad with the Queen to-day
to Durdan's, it seems to dine with my Lord Berkely at
his seat near Epsom, where I have been very merry
when I was a little boy." There was evidently a building
called Durdans when Pepys was " a little boy," so that
several facts demonstrate that the original house cannot
have been the one built by Lord Berkeley. The fact
that Pepys spells the name Durdan's seems to point to
an owner of some former house, the practice of calling
the house after its owner having been so common in
the past. Charles II *dined* at Durdans, but there is no
authority for stating that he slept there, although if he
stopped at Epsom for the night he would most likely
have chosen Durdans. Under the date of August 4th,
1665, Evelyn again writes : " On my return from
Wotton (whither he had taken his son and tutor for fear
of the Plague) I call'd at Durdans, where I found
Dr. Wilkins, Sir Wm. Petty, and Mr. Hooke, contriving
Chariots, new rigging for ships, a wheele for one to
run races in, and other mechanical inventions ; perhaps
three such persons together were not to be found
elsewhere in Europe, for parts and ingenuity."

John Aubrey, who dearly loved to quote scandal,
writing of Durdans (the Nonsuch building) says it

"is built *à la modern,* the front to the Downs and the other to the gardens are very regular and noble ; but what has rendered it more famous of late years is the beautiful Grove, the Scene of Love between *Ford,* Lord *Grey* of *Werk* and his Lady's sister (Henrietta, daughter of the Earl of Berkeley), a fatal and almost unheard of passion." In Manning and Bray's History of Surrey this statement is corrected on the authority of the Rev. John Parkhurst, the scene of the scandal being at the other seat of Lord Berkeley, where the present work-house stands on the Dorking Road. Lord Grey of Werk was prosecuted with others who were conspiring with him to seduce the lady from Durdans, her father's house, but although found guilty no judgment was recorded against them. Writing of the trial, Macaulay says : "A scene unparalleled in our legal history was exhibited in the Court of King's Bench. The seducer appeared with dauntless front, accompanied by his paramour. Nor did the great Whig Lords flinch from their friend's side even in that extremity. Those whom he had wronged stood over against him, and were moved to transports of rage by the sight of him. The old Earl of Berkeley poured forth reproaches and curses on the wretched Henrietta. The Countess gave evidence, broken by many sobs, and at length fell down in a swoon. The jury found a verdict of guilty. When the Court rose, Lord Berkeley called on all his friends to help him to seize his daughter. The partisans of Grey rallied round her. Swords were drawn on both sides ; a skirmish took place in Westminster Hall, and it was with difficulty that the judges and tipstaves parted the combatants." In the records of the evidence given at the trial, dated 1720, it plainly appears that Lord Berkeley's family resided " at Durdants (*sic*) near Epsom, at the time of this ill accident."

Durdans was sold by Lord Berkeley's heirs to John, Duke of Argyll and Greenwich, and prior to December, 1737, it became the property of Lord North and Guilford. Between the years 1737 and 1747 Durdans was for a time chosen as his residence by Frederick, Prince of Wales, father of George III. There is

authority for this in one of Horace Walpole's letters to
Richard Bentley, dated February 23, 1755, when he
writes, "There have been two more great fires. Alderman Belchier's house at Epsom that belonged to the
Prince [of Wales] is burnt."   Despite the exalted
character given him by Hume, the historian, the
concensus of opinion seems to have considered Frederick,
Prince of Wales, "a poor, weak, irresolute, false,

FREDERICK, PRINCE OF WALES,
Who at one time resided at Durdans.

lying, dishonest, contemptible wretch."   Among his
other amusements Prince Frederick was devoted to
hawking, a spot once known as the Hawkery on the
Downs being connected with this sport.   At this time
there was a fine grove of walnut trees nearly a quarter
of a mile long, running from the house (or palace as it
is called by Toland and others) to the Common Fields
which occupied the space between the present day
Alexandra and Downs Roads.   In old maps, Downs

Road, or what nearly approximated to it, was known as Walnut Tree Road from the grove cut down in the early years of the nineteenth century. Where the grove terminated, there stood, until the year 1824, an obelisk placed there by Prince Frederick. Swete gives the following account of the circumstances leading to its erection, for which there is no other known authority. " As Frederick was walking early in the morning by himself, he saw, sitting at the end of the avenue, a sweep dark with the soot of his vocation. Angry at his intrusion into the Royal grounds, the Prince called on him to begone. The merriest of grins was the only reply. A walking-stick was quickly flourished over the intruder, but as quickly wrenched from the Royal hand. After some angry words, the sweep dared Frederick to the fight, and having stripped his sooty body, he stood fronting the heir of England's throne. Nothing loath to this new adventure, Frederick threw off his coat, and set to fisticuffs with his antagonist, who being a hardy boxer, succeeded in bringing the fight to a conclusion sadly adverse to the Prince. He trod on the neck of his fallen enemy and loudly proclaimed himself victor. Frederick had the magnanimity, not only to confess his defeat, but to reward his conqueror, and often told the story with much grace, while he ordered the obelisk to be erected in honour of the fight."

When the obelisk was removed, the present Parish Church was being erected, and the flints of which it was composed were incorporated into the walls of the new building.

It was in 1747 that Alderman Belchier had the estate, and it was he who for some unknown reason took down the fine old house built by the Earl of Berkeley, of which a painting is still in existence. Before the new building was finished it was accidentally burnt down in 1755.

Finally the existing house of red brick and stone was built in 1764 and purchased by a Mr. Dalbiac ; it passed to Mr. George Blackman in 1799 who sold it in 1819 to Sir Gilbert Heathcote, Bart., M.P. for the county of Rutland, the property descending to his son, Arthur

MR. ARTHUR HEATHCOTE,
Who succeeded his father, Sir Gilbert Heathcote, in the ownership of Durdans.
From an old Drawing.

Heathcote, who died, and from whose cousins and heirs Lord Rosebery purchased it in 1874. Lord Rosebery has made considerable alterations, including a new entrance hall near the stables and the blocking up of the former one.

The situation of the house on undulating ground flanked by huge trees is very fortunate, while the gardens towards the south lose themselves in a dark strip of woodland in a particularly fascinating manner. At the sides of the gravel walks there are quite a number of yews clipped into all sorts of quaint forms after the attractive style of Dutch gardening.

Facing the road by Woodcote Green there are some picturesque little cottages, a large barn, and a white stuccoed house, the residence of Mrs. Kennerley Rumford—in 1825 occupied by Mr. Richard Harvey and described by Pownall as "an elegant villa replete with comfort." At the corner of the Green, facing three old limes, is a very charming old house with dormer windows in the roof and a wide gable behind. It is known as Woodcote Green House and is occupied by Mrs. Buller. The nearest house to this is Woodcote Place—Mr. A. E. Harter's—at one time the residence of Sir John Jackson. The adjoining house towards the town—it is separated by a little inn and one or two cottages—is Woodcote End House, and its fine old red brick walls and semi-circular porch are at once noticeable. Here, about the year 1780, lived the Rev. Martin Madan, a celebrated preacher and writer. He was born in 1726 at Hertingfordbury near Hertford, his father being groom of the bedchamber to Frederick, Prince of Wales, while his mother was daughter of Spencer Cowper and niece of the Lord Chancellor Cowper. Martin Madan eventually became a popular preacher at the Lock Hospital Chapel in London, but after the publication in 1780 of his famous book, "Thelyphthora," through which he was unjustly accused of countenancing polygamy, he retired from the pulpit. While living at Epsom he used his authority as a magistrate to prevent illegal games in the town during race week. His

The Rev. Martin Madan.

success in this matter so infuriated the townsfolk that they burnt him in effigy in the High Street where one of the pumps now stands. Mr. Madan died at Epsom in 1790, and his memory is preserved in Madan's Lane, a footpath leading from Woodcote Green to the fields by the Ashley Road.

Facing the end of Worple Road where it enters Woodcote, there stand some exceedingly pretty cream-washed cottages covered with flowering creepers and with roses trained round their antique little leaded windows, while a few yards towards Chalk Lane, surrounded and overshadowed by trees, is the "Amato" Inn pictured here. Before Amato won the Derby in 1838, this was known as "The Hare and Hounds." The odd medley of its tiled roofs, its painted wooden walls, and the well outside surrounded by one or two long out-of-date chaises and gigs, are the features most noticeable as one passes beneath its bright red sign-board.

A little further on, Woodcote Grove faces the turning leading to Durdans. There is no doubt at all that this is what Toland refers to as Mount Diston in his "Letter to Eudoxa" already quoted. He says, "The other house in Epsom that requires a special mention, is Mount Diston, so nam'd from the owner, and from the round hillock near adjoining, which, rising gently on all sides in a conic figure, terminates on the summit in a circle, which is a hundred foot diameter, and divided into four equal quarters. The round and cross walks of this circle are turf'd, and those triangular quarters planted with trees; which, after they are grown to their full height, will make a stately landmark over all this country. But tho' nothing seems more pleasing to the eye, than the near prospect of the town, or the distant prospect quite around, yet you mount still higher nine and twenty steps into an arbour or pavilion, on the top of an oak, that grows in the very edge of the circle, and whence your view is every way proportionably enlarg'd. Up to this circle there comes a double walk, divided by a range of trees from the best garden, yet of very easy

Woodcote Grove.

THE "AMATO" INN AT WOODCOTE.

Before "Amato" won the Derby in 1838, this was known as the "Hare and Hounds."

ascent, three hundred and fifty-five foot, which I call the north walk : and at the other end, there comes up to it likewise from the reservatory the south walk, three hundred and seventy foot ; in both which the slopes seem wonderfully natural, yet artfully contrived. At the foot of the mount is a cross walk, from north-east to south-west, two hundred and ten foot, open at each end thro' handsom grills ; and from the court before the house there goes a walk from north-west to south-east, five hundred and fifty-five foot, including the

THE 17TH CENTURY FIREGRATE IN THE ENTRANCE HALL
OF WOODCOTE GROVE.

breadth of court. Behind the house is a magnificent double terrass, the middle of each being gravel, and turf on the sides, (which may be adorn'd with evergreen dwarfs) three hundred foot long ; and the semi-circular slope, with proper squares, in the middle of this terrass, is eighty foot broad : to which you ascend out of the garden ten steps, being five steps to each terrass, and then ten steps more from the upper terrass into the house ; all these steps, as well as those in the fore-court, being of excellent Portland stone."

WOODCOTE GROVE,
Built about 1680 by Alderman Diston.

These paths and measurements have been found to be substantially correct, forming ample evidence for stating that Woodcote Grove was formerly Mount Diston. Mr. Josiah Diston, who was one of the early Governors of the Bank of England, seems to have built the house for himself some time during the reign Charles II, and through expensive living and possibly some gaming, he entirely ruined himself, selling the property to a Mr. Garland, the great grandfather of the present Mr. E. W. Garland, who states that the house has been much altered by his father within his own memory, Mr. A. W. Aston who now resides there having carried out further alterations. From the time the Garlands had the property, the place was generally spoken of as " Garland's," so that in time people began to imagine that the house had been given that name. Mr. Garland has, at his London house, a painting of Mr. Diston, probably by Sir Peter Lely, and one of Charles II which came out of Woodcote Grove—sold, doubtless, at the same time as the house, for it is understood that the owner was really ruined. As it stands to-day Woodcote Grove is a well designed and conspicuously attractive house. It is constructed of red and yellow brick with bright green jalousie shutters—a note of colour seldom striven for and still more rarely attained. The dining room has Mr. Diston's original floor inlaid with dark red tulip wood, and the entrance hall has a fine old fire-grate dating from the 17th century. Some of the walls are remarkable, those of the circular staircase being five feet, six inches thick. But still more astonishing are the huge vault-like cellars beneath the drive in front of the house and also at the back. They are far too commodious for ordinary purposes and their curious recesses and alcoves seem to point unerringly to the smuggling days when such quantities of " run " goods found their way up the Portsmouth Road and into the houses of so many Surrey towns. Some of the bedrooms have small alcoves, which were probably used for powdering. From the back of Woodcote Grove runs a fine double avenue of elms, terminating at a bend in the Worple Road, but whether

this was ever connected with any of the other avenues
in the town it is impossible to say.

On the south side of the Dorking Road stands
Hylands House, a high brick house,
picturesquely covered with ivy, the residence
of the Hon. Sir Thomas T. Bucknill, Judge
of the High Court. Many years ago this house
belonged to Richard Starke, who was for some time
Governor of Fort St. George, Madras, and whose
daughter Mariana was famous for her guide books.
Her early years were spent in India, and her keen
observation of Anglo-Indian life supplied material for
her comedy, "The Sword of Peace, or a Voyage of
Love," acted at the Haymarket Theatre in 1788 with
Miss Farren in the cast. Miss Starke having spent
several years in Italy published "The Beauties of Carlo
Maria Maggi Paraphrased," "Travels on the Continent,"
and "Travels in Europe for the use of Travellers on
the Continent and likewise in the island of Sicily, to
which is added an account of the Remains of Ancient
Italy." Her works were carefully compiled and proved
useful forerunners of the labours of Murray and
Baedeker. Subsequent to Governor Starke, a certain
Lady Duckingfield lived in Hylands House. Adjoining
it on either side are two houses of considerable antiquity
and architectural interest, with the curiously similar
names of Hylands and The Hylands.

Approaching the town one passes some cottages and
an inn on the right, and a little further on the same side,
standing back from the road, are the extensive red brick
buildings of the Workhouse, standing on the site of a
mansion said to have belonged at one time to the Earls
of Berkeley. Close to the workhouse gates is the
pound with its ancient oaken fencing.

The very substantial stuccoed house opposite, the
residence of Mr. M. E. Muir, and often
spoken of as "The Clock House," is really
named The Elms. Toland speaks of this as "Mr.
Rooth's in New Inn Lane" (see page 53), and the canal
he refers to is doubtless the strip of water at the end
of the grounds. Sir John Brewer Davis afterwards

held the property, selling it eventually to a corn chandler of Epsom, named Cunningham. This man ruined himself through his rash purchase and, becoming a bankrupt, he divided the land and pulled down the greater part of the house, disposing of the estate to Sir James Alexander, who practically rebuilt the house in its present form. Two large houses, it is said, stood facing the Elms, but they had disappeared altogether in 1825.

Abele Grove was at one time, according to Brayley, the residence of Sir William Parsons and then "a place of much grandeur." Early in the nineteenth century the property belonged to Mr. John Pugh, who improved the house after a period of ruinous neglect. The grounds include the rounded hill overlooking South Street, conspicuous for its large trees whose upper branches have been sawn off.

On Clay hill—deriving its name from the nature of its soil—is Hookfield, formerly known as Hookfield Grove. The present house of white brick was built by Mr. James Levick about 1860, and was in 1868 sold to Mr. Isaac Braithwaite, father of the present Mr. Basil Braithwaite. The first house was that mentioned by Toland as "Sir John Ward's house on Clay Hill." This was afterwards inhabited by a Mr. Knipe.

Horton Lodge, standing on the high ground above Christ Church, belongs to Mr. Henry Willis. A former house belonged to Charles Browning, son of the Hon. Louisa Browning, who was sister of Lord Baltimore.

Close to the Parish Church of Epsom stands Pit Place, belonging to Mr. W. E. Bagshaw,
Pit Place. an exceptionally interesting house on account of the quantity of carved stonework brought from Nonsuch Palace and also for its holding the room in which the dissolute Thomas, second Baron Lyttelton, died under such portentous circumstances.

Pit Place was, it seems, originally a small farmhouse, standing in a huge chalk pit, and various owners added to it in such a manner as to make one of the most unusually arranged dwellings in Epsom. The central portion has comparatively low ceilings and walls of prodigious thickness, while the drawing room is

THE BEDROOM IN PIT PLACE,

In which Lord Lyttelton died three days after his
statement relating to the apparition.

extremely lofty with walls of moderate proportions. Much of the interior woodwork is richly carved, especially in the bedroom in which Lord Lyttelton died, where grotesque masks and fretted panels are inserted around the windows and doors. The alcove behind the curtains shown in the drawing reproduced here, was in Lord Lyttelton's time shut off by folding doors, but otherwise the room is practically untouched, although there is unfortunately none of the old furniture left. It was on Nov. 26th, 1779, that Lord Lyttelton terminated his career at Pit Place, and the circumstances attending it are so remarkable that I quote at length the account written by a gentleman who was visiting him at the time :—

" I was at Pit Place, Epsom, when Lord Lyttelton died. Lord Fortescue, Lady Flood, and the two Miss Amphletts, were also present. Lord Lyttelton had not long been returned from Ireland, and frequently had been seized with suffocating fits; he was attacked several times by them in the course of the preceding month, while he was at his house in Hill Street, Berkeley Square. It happened that he dreamt, three days before his death, that he saw a fluttering bird, and afterwards that a Woman appeared to him in white apparel, and said to him, ' Prepare to die ; you will not exist three days.' His lordship was much alarmed, and called to a servant from a closet adjoining, who found him much agitated, and in a profuse perspiration : the circumstance had a considerable effect all the next day on his lordship's spirits. On the third day, while his lordship was at breakfast with the above personages, he said, ' If I live over to-night, I shall have jockied the ghost, for this is the third day.' The whole party presently set off for Pit Place, where they had not long arrived before his lordship was visited by one of his accustomed fits : after a short interval he recovered. He dined at five o'clock that day, and went to bed at eleven, when his servant was about to give him rhubarb and mint-water ; but his lordship, perceiving him stirring it with a toothpick, called him a slovenly dog, and bid him go and fetch a teaspoon. On the man's return he found his master in a fit, and the pillow being placed high, his

G

chin bore hard upon his neck: when the servant, instead of relieving his lordship on the instant from his perilous situation, ran, in his fright, and called out for help; but on his return he found his lordship dead."

Commenting on this account, Brayley adds: "In explanation of this strange tale, it is said that Lord Lyttelton acknowledged, previously to his death, that the woman he had seen in his dream was the mother of the two Miss Amphletts mentioned above; whom, together with a third sister, then in Ireland, his lordship had seduced, and prevailed on to leave their parent, who resided near his country seat in Shropshire. It is further stated, that Mrs. Amphlett died of grief, through the desertion of her children, at the precise time when the female vision appeared to his lordship; and that, about the period of his own dissolution, a personage answering his description visited the bed-side of the late Miles Peter Andrews, Esq., who had been friend and companion of Lord Lyttelton in his revels, and suddenly throwing open the curtains, desired Mr. Andrews to come to him. The latter, not knowing that his lordship had

A CARVED STONE FIGURE,

Forming the side of a fireplace in one of the upper rooms of Pit Place, presumably from Nonsuch Palace.

returned from Ireland, suddenly got up, when the phantom disappeared. Mr. Andrews frequently declared that the alarm caused him to have a short fit of illness; and, in his subsequent visits to Pit Place, no solicitations could ever induce him to take a bed there; but he would invariably return, however late, to the Spread Eagle Inn at Epsom for the night."

In a room on the first floor there are two carved stone Elizabethan or Early Jacobean figures, palpably out of place in their surroundings. These, together with the two lions on the pillars of the stable gateway, the carved head inserted in the gable end of the stables, and the many pieces of carved stone distributed over the rockeries in the garden, all seem to have come from Nonsuch Palace. Some fine cedars and many other trees grow upon the terraced sides of the pit, pierced in three or four places with curious tunnels, one of them passing beneath the road at the back of the garden, and emerging close to a neighbouring cottage. In the volume entitled "Passages from the Diary of Mrs. Phillip Lybbe Powys," edited by Emily J. Climenson, there is a reference to what must be Pit Place, as there is no other house in Epsom at all answering to the description. "She visits in 1759, from her relation, Mr. Mount's place at Epsom, Lord Baltimore's seat, a Mr. Belchier's also, which she describes as very curious —'literally contained within the circumference of a chalk-pit. Its owner had a very fine seat called Durdens, in Surrey, burnt to the ground; but instead of rebuilding that, has collected not only the necessaries, but even the luxuries of life into the above small compass—a good house, one room 30 feet by 20 and 15 feet high. In his gardens (all within the pit) is hothouse, green-house, orangery, vinery, pinery, a grove, terrace, fish-ponds, fountain with rock-work, and the largest gold and silver fish I ever saw, a hot and cold bath, a pretty shrubbery; in short, one cannot name anything that is not in this wonderful chalk-pit.'" The carved stone-work, reputed to have been brought from Nonsuch Palace, may therefore have been brought from Durdans by Mr. Belchier. Nearly opposite Pit Place, in Church Street, is Ebbisham House, a large, old-fashioned, rectangular brick house, absolutely devoid of any ornament except that contributed by a fine growth of ivy and the action of the weather.

Nearer the town on the same side of the road is

Parkhurst, a building similar in style to Ebbisham House, but set sideways to the road. A little further on is the Vicarage of St. Martin's Church, a red brick house containing a fine staircase similar in pattern to that in Silver Birches, the residence of Dr. W. Clement Daniel. Both of the balustrades of these staircases are believed to have been brought from Nonsuch. Opposite the Vicarage and hiding itself successfully from the gaze of passers-by, is the Grove, occupied about sixty years ago by Mr. John Whitmore, a Governor of the Bank of England, and now by the Misses Pye-mont. The grounds are fortunate in possessing numbers of fine trees, and these, in conjunction with the high red brick walls, keep the grounds quite secluded although so close to the centre of the town.

The Cedars, at the corner of the Worple Road, is named from the two trees standing sentinels just out-side the iron gates. They are a beautiful feature of Church Street, and may be seen from a fair distance in both directions. The house of brick is old, ivy clad, and low, the parapets being ornamented with stone balls. The next house is Silver Birches, just mentioned. It is probably as old as any house in Epsom, and contains a considerable amount of panelling and other woodwork, as well as some antique paintings of mythical subjects, probably from Nonsuch. An interesting discovery was made some years ago in the room to the left of the entrance hall. The panelling between the fire-place and one of the windows having been removed, a hollow space was found, containing a trap-door in the floor, leading to a cellar below. From the cellar, a passage ran in the direction of the roadway. There seems little doubt that the cellar and the passage were, like those at Woodcote Grove, built for smuggling purposes. Many years ago some early eighteenth century invitation cards to chocolate at the "Albion" and similar functions were discovered on removing some old panelling.

The Acacias, facing the Worple Road, is a lovely old house with cream-washed walls and a steep tiled roof—it has been mentioned before in connection with Sir John Hartopp and Dr. Isaac Watts.

CHAPTER VI.

CONCERNING SOME WORTHIES
OF EPSOM.

SO many personages of varying degrees of historic importance have lived in Epsom, that to give a separate account of each would fill many volumes. I have therefore been obliged to refer briefly to most of the notable residents in the chapter dealing with the houses in which they dwelt.

The White House, or, as it was formerly known, Haswell House, in Waterloo Road, was for a time, according to Swete's Handbook of Epsom, published about forty years ago, the abode of the Prince of Wales (afterwards George IV) and his much-injured wife, Mrs. Fitzherbert. It is a quaint and picturesque house, looking smaller than it really is on account of its being a little lower than the level of the road. Before the railway came, the views from the windows across the meadows towards Horton must have been very charming, but now they are limited to the station and embankment of the South Western Railway. In the memoirs of Mrs. Fitzherbert by the Hon. Charles Langdale (1856), there is no reference to Epsom, but so very few details of places are given there that one need not, on that account, consider it a mere fable. Lord Stourton in his narrative of the intercourse between Mrs. Fitzherbert and the Prince, says that for several years they were extremely poor, and on one occasion, when returning from Brighton to London, they mustered their common means and

[marginal note:] George IV and Mrs. Fitzherbert.

could not raise £5 between them. The size of the
house, therefore, need not be considered an obstacle
to the acceptance of the statement of the old guide
book writer.

This same authority points out the "White House"
as being at a later period the residence
of Sharon Turner. William Jerdan in his
"Men I have known," says, "Once, when
I went to see him in a quiet retreat from the busy

Sharon
Turner.

THE PRINCE OF WALES, AFTERWARDS GEORGE IV.
Who is believed to have stopped at Epsom with Mrs. Fitzherbert.

world, at Epsom, he gave me a volume of which few
of my readers have probably heard;" but beyond this
I have been unable to trace any further reference to
Epsom. That Turner lived in Epsom is a fact, and
that he lived in the "White House" is exceedingly
probable, Swete's Handbook being published so near
to the period of the author's fame that a mistake was
not likely to occur.

Sharon Turner was born in Pentonville on Sept. 24th,
1768. His parents were Yorkshire people, who had
come to London on their marriage. They entrusted
Sharon's education to Dr. James Davies, whose academy
was at Pentonville, and when he was fifteen articled
him to an attorney in the Temple. Six years later,
in 1789, his master having died without an heir, Sharon
was enabled to carry on the business with the help of

some of the leading clients. He married in 1795, and settled in Red Lion Square. When still quite a boy his attention was attracted to the old northern literature by a translation of the "Death song of Ragnar Lodbrok," and from that time forward he began the study of Icelandic and Anglo-Saxon, and in time every moment he could spare from his professional work he devoted to study at the British Museum. It was with some surprise that he discovered how little the ancient materials had been used by historians such as Hume (1761). Sharon Turner was the first to explore, for historical purposes, the Anglo-Saxon manuscripts in the Cottonian Library. In 1799, after sixteen years of study, he produced the first portion of his "History of England from the earliest period to the Norman Conquest." The work was a complete revelation, receiving the commendation of Palgrave in the "Edinburgh Review," and Southey was of opinion "that so much information was probably never laid before the public in one historical publication."

Having decided to continue the history, Turner produced between 1814 and 1823 his "History of England from the Norman Conquest to 1509," following the same independent lines in his researches. In 1826 he added the "Reign of Henry VIII," partly with a view to controverting some of the positions taken by Lingard, whose History of England in eight volumes appeared just before this time.

Finally Turner added the reigns of Edward VI, Mary, and Elizabeth—the whole of these histories being eventually issued in twelve octavo volumes as "The History of England from the earliest time to the death of Queen Elizabeth." So much did the latter part of the history fall below the standard of the pre-Norman portion that even Southey was altered in his opinion and pronounced with frankness that he wished the style had been less ambitious. "His views had little originality and his treatment of his subject had no superior merit," says Thomas Seccombe in the Dictionary of National Biography.

After the heavy labour entailed by these works,

Turner, in 1829, retired from business and settled at Winchmore Hill, and from there he issued the first volume of the "Sacred History of the World as displayed in the Creation and subsequent Events to the Deluge, attempted to be philosophically considered in a series of letters to a son." It became very popular, largely owing to the thoroughly orthodox spirit in which it was written. "We would refer the ladies of Epsom," says Swete quaintly, in his eulogistic reference to the historian, "to that beautiful passage in the 'History of the Creation,' where he thus wrote, with the experience of seventy summers to mature his judgment, 'one of the most beautiful, interesting, and benevolent ideas of the Divine mind, in His creation of the terrestrial economy was the conception and formation of the female sex. No other production has contributed so much to the improvement and happiness of human nature.'"

For many years Sharon Turner was closely associated with John Murray the publisher, who frequently consulted him on legal matters concerning copyright, particularly in connection with the literary outlaw "Don Juan;" and in the starting of the "Quarterly" Turner deprecated the tendency to imitate the smart style of the "Edinburgh Review," and urged that "harmless, inoffensive work" should be compassionately treated. The early numbers of the "Quarterly" contained two or three of Turner's articles.

His wife, who was described as "beautiful, accomplished, and agreeable," died in 1843, and on February 13th, 1847, Turner breathed his last in his son's house in Red Lion Square, London. During the last twelve years of his life, Turner, who was an F.S.A. as well as an Associate of the Royal Society of Literature, received a Civil List pension of £300 a year.

Macaulay quotes him, and Hallam, Southey, Scott, and Tennyson all had a lasting interest in Sharon Turner, for although his critical power may have been defective, he certainly possessed a remarkable power of presentation. Speaking of his personal qualities, Jerdan says, "If you wish to know something of the man, I can only tell you that he was simple, as all truly wise men are, unassuming, genial, laborious, and conscientious."

At the time of the decline of the Wells as a popular resort, a very grotesque figure appeared at Epsom. She is generally known as Mrs. Mapp the "Bone-setter" or "Shape-mistress." Her father, whose name was Wallin, was a bone-setter at Hindon in Wiltshire. Manning calls her the "sister of that Polly Peachum who was married to the Duke of Bolton," but Brayley proves this to be an error. Leaving her father's house

Mrs. Mapp, the Bone Setter.

MRS. MAPP, THE REMARKABLE BONE-SETTER OF EPSOM.

From Hogarth's Picture, "The Undertakers' Arms."

Mrs. Mapp is the centre figure. She is for some obscure reason shown in a harlequin's attire.

on account of some quarrel, Sally Wallin wandered from place to place, calling herself Crazy Sally and affecting insanity. Her rambles brought her to Epsom, and her skill in setting disjointed limbs soon spread to London, for in the *Gentleman's Magazine* of July, 1736 (p. 422), she is mentioned as a "strolling woman, now at *Epsom*, who calls herself *Crazy Sally*; and had perform'd cures in Bone-setting to admiration and occasion'd so great a resort, that the town offered her

100 Guineas to continue there a year." Another reference (in August, 1736) says, " The cures performed by the woman Bonesetter of *Epsom* are too many to be enumerated : Her Bandages are extraordinary neat, and her dexterity in reducing dislocations and setting of fractured Bones wonderful. . . . The money she got procured her a Husband ; but he did not stay with her above a Fortnight, and then went off with 100 guineas." This husband was a Mr. Hill Mapp, a footman to a mercer on Ludgate Hill. The Epsom people were much against the match and did all they could to prevent it, either knowing Mapp to be a scoundrel or fearing that she would be induced to leave Epsom. When the day appointed for the marriage arrived, Sally Wallin refused to restore a child's dislocated neck until she became Mrs. Mapp. Sir James Edwards of Walton-on-Thames, who had brought the child, lent her his carriage in order to drive to Ewell where she hoped to find a conveyance to London. On being disappointed she decided to be married at Headley, but on passing near Epsom the coachman refused to drive her further, so she alighted and entered a cottage where a deputation of Epsom ladies came out to intreat her to return. It was no avail and the headstrong woman started off to walk to Banstead church (presumably with Mr. Mapp). A number of people drove after her, and on finding that the minister had no license, a Mr. Bridgewater who felt considerably for the poor people who were waiting to be cured at Epsom, drove her to London in his chariot bringing her back immediately afterwards.

Not long after her marriage Mrs. Mapp left Epsom and took lodgings in Pall Mall, but on December 10th, 1737, scarcely sixteen months later, she died "at her lodgings near Seven Dials, so miserably poor that the parish were obliged to bury her."

On one occasion, it is said, some surgeons who doubted her skill sent an impostor to have his wrist set. Mrs. Mapp found the limb quite sound, but by giving it a sudden wrench, she actually put it out of joint and told him "to go to the fools who sent him, and get his wrist set again ; or if he would come that day month she would do it herself." In a little publication entitled "Leatherhead and its Legends," the Rev. S. N. Sedgwick has woven an account of this remarkable woman into a very absorbing little narrative. It is not all fact, but it illumines the period in a remarkable way.

John Toland, to whom we owe that valuable account

John Toland. of Epsom at the commencement of the eighteenth century quoted in a previous chapter, took a house on Woodcote Green in 1710. Whether the house still stands or where it stood is unknown. The only building at all possible seems to be Woodcote Green House.

Toland was born near Londonderry in 1670. His true name was Janus Junius Toland, but to avoid ridicule it is said that his schoolmaster altered it to John. Although brought up as a Catholic, he became a Protestant before he was sixteen, and soon after his abilities attracted the notice of some "eminent dissenters" who educated him as a minister. In 1687 he went to college at Glasgow and in 1690 was created M.A. at Edinburgh University. He continued his studies at Leyden, where he is described as a "student in divinity," and two years later went to Oxford. In 1696 his "Christianity not Mysterious" caused considerable controversy. It was the opening of the warfare betwen deists and the orthodox party which continued for a generation. Through injudicious talk in coffee-houses and public places Toland, as a deist, was soon subject to much persecution. Shortly after this he edited Milton's prose works and prefixed a life, also separately published.

From about 1718 Toland lived at Putney. At length in 1721 his health began to fail, and having composed a Latin epitaph for himself a few days before, he died after much patient suffering on March 11th, 1721-2.

A little cottage near the South Western Station and

Leigh Hunt. immediately adjoining the archway through which the footpath leads to Horton, was, it is stated, often visited by Leigh Hunt.

CHAPTER VII.

HOW THE DOWNS BECAME FAMOUS FOR HORSE-RACING.

THERE seems little doubt that James I, during his occasional residences at Nonsuch Palace, held the earliest horse races on Epsom Downs, in those days called Banstead Downs. It was for foot races, however, that they first became famous,

The Origin of the Races. Pepys in his diary referring to them as being frequently held. In those days every family of importance had one or more "running footmen," and it became a common practice to set them to run races.

The suitability of the ground, with its short close turf, seems to have made the Downs a permanently favoured spot, for during the time of the Commonwealth horse races were held frequently enough to be used as a cloak for the meeting of large bodies of Royalists. Clarendon in his "History of the Rebellion" says, "Soon after the meeting which was held at Guildford, 18th May, 1648, to address the two houses of Parliament, that the King, their only lawful Sovereign, might be restored to his due honours . . . . a meeting of the Royalists was held on Banstead (Epsom) Downs under the pretence of a horse race, and six hundred horse were collected and marched to Reigate."

At the Restoration came the immense popularity of Epsom as a watering place, and the throng of fashionable people naturally seized upon the races as an excellent means of passing their long days of idleness

The races were now and had been for some time con-
ducted nearly in the same style in essentials as the
present day, but a silver bell was usually the prize.
The origin of this custom is given in Hone's "Every
day Book." "In 1609 or 1610, Mr. William Lester,
mercer, being Mayor of Chester, did cause three silver
bells to be made, of good value, which bells he appointed
to be run for with horses." An excellent picture of the
Downs on Race days as long ago as 1735 can be
conjured up from the *Bath, Bristol, Tunbridge and
Epsom Miscellany*. The lines are by an anonymous
writer :—

> On Epsom Downs when Racing does begin,
> Large companies from every part come in,
> Tag rag and Bob-tail, Lords and Ladies meet,
> And, Squires without Estates, each other greet.
> A scoundrel here, pray take it on my Word,
> Is a companion for the greatest Lord,
> Provided that his Purse abounds with Gold,
> If not, then this Affection will not hold.
> Here the promiscuous and ungovern'd Crew
> Crowd to see what is neither strange or new ;
> Bets upon Bets, this Man says—two to one,
> Another pointing cries, good Sir, 'tis done.
> See how they gallop o'er the spacious Plain,
> As if pursu'd, and dreading to be slain ;
> Not half such speed would any of them make,
> To save their Country if she lay at Stake.
> The Races done, to Town the mob repair,
> Some curse their Fate, and some the Booty share.

The "Peace of Paris," which closed the Seven Years'
War in 1763, gave rise to a meeting of eight gentlemen
of Surrey on the Downs, but it was not
with the object of witnessing races. The
meeting was fixed by public advertisement
for the 7th of July, 1763, and it was
considered extraordinary because the body
of the county were to meet at the Assizes
so soon afterwards as the 27th. It was to discuss the
terms of the Peace with France that these worthy
gentlemen met, and the circumstances attending it
were given in "'The Battle of Epsom,' a new Ballad.
1763 Bella, horrida Bella, virg."

*A Meeting
of Surrey
Gentlemen
on the
Downs.*

COURSING ON EPSOM DOWNS. *Photographed by J. G. Tillett, of Epsom.*

From an old coloured Print in the possession of Mr. A. W. Aston.

Ye good men of Surrey, both ancient and young,
All loyal and true, pray attend to my Song ;
I sing, tho' the *Scotchmen* should smile or should frown,
The wonderful Feats done at *Epsom* fair Town,
    Derry down, down, down, derry down.

How *Eight English* worthies a meeting desired,
To address to the *Peace* by their duty inspired,
Tho' Scandal has said, with a very ill grace,
Some wanted to *keep,* others *get—a good place.*
    Derry down, &c.

But Mawbey, who heard of their plan, and could guess,
Set engines to work to prevent their success ;
To his firm *Borough* Friends his objections made known,
Who vowed to go with him to *Epsom* fair Town.
    Derry down, &c.

At fair *Epsom* arrived, see, the Enemy near,
Survey with Concern, as awaken'd by Fear,
Some think of the Combat, of others the Aim,
Was—only to steal away just as they came.
    Derry down, &c.

Northey, Godsehall and Tucker, their fears making known,
Did not like the Appearance, so wished to *postpone ;*
But Talbot, the furious, and dull, won't agree,
And *Geary,* the valiant, cry'd, Sirs, it shan't be.
    Derry down, &c.

The Troops all drawn up, *Mawbey* 'gan the Attack,
And *Northey* and *Godsehall* were forc'd to draw back ;
Their Quarters, were ta'en by Surprise and Neglect,
O'erthrown by a Weapon they did not expect.
    Derry down, &c.

There are many other verses giving Sir Joseph Mawbey's arguments which finally led to the abandonment of the meeting.

Hawking was at one time a common practice on the Downs, where there was once a spot known as "The Hawkery.' Races have been held on the Downs, annually, since 1730, but their immense popularity after the decline of Epsom as a watering place did not commence until 1779. In that year the "Oaks" was instituted, receiving its name from "The Oaks," the seat of the Earl of Derby at Banstead. The "Derby," deriving its name from the same great patron of the turf, was first run in 1780. Between the Grand Stand and Sherwood's stables traces of

Institution of the "Oaks" and the "Derby."

the old betting ring may be seen on the turf, while
the position of the "ride," the "Rotten Row" of
Epsom in its palmy days, is indicated by the more vivid
greenness of the grass between the Grand Stand, the
"Derby Arms" and the rifle butts.

At the end of the eighteenth century meetings of the
Royal Surrey Bowmen used to take place on Epsom
Downs. A print of one of the meetings of these archers
is given in the *Home Counties' Magazine* for October,
1900. It was in 1828 that a Doncaster man named

The
Grand
Stand.

Charles Bluck applied for an acre of land
on which to erect a Grand Stand. Having
permission from the Lord of the Manor the
present building was constructed in 1829,
at a cost of £20,000. In 1886 it was considerably
enlarged, and another addition was only finished in
1900. Her late Majesty Queen Victoria on her visit to
the Epsom Races with Prince Albert in 1840, drove
through a grassy avenue in Woodcote Park, reaching
the Downs in privacy, and at the same time enjoying
the rich scenery of the Park.

The breezy slopes of the Downs are invaded by the mot-
ley crowds at two seasons of the year, for the "Spring"
meeting, and at the end of May or the beginning of
June for the "Derby." An autumn meeting was tried
for a few years, but has been abandoned.

For weeks before the date of the races the pic-

The
Invasion
of Gipsies.

turesque but unsavoury collection of gipsy
encampments commence to accumulate on
the portion of the Downs allotted to them.
The caravans come from the remotest
corners of England, some of the swarthy occupants
having remarkably Egyptian features. Special police-
men are told off to prevent disturbances among the
nomads, and every one of them is obliged to leave the
Downs during the day following the races.

Great care is taken by the Urban District Council to

Epsom on
Race Days.

prevent infectious diseases from being im-
ported into the town during the incursion
of the unholy mob, and the streets are
frequently watered with disinfectants.

Photographed by Chester Vaughan.

THE GRAND STAND

The scene in front of the Grand Stand on Epsom Downs on a "Derby" Day.

H

People on foot and in small traps begin to arrive as early as eight in the morning, and by ten an almost continuous stream of vehicles raise clouds of white dust over each of the approaches to the Downs. Later on the roads become one solid line of coaches, brakes, wagonettes and miscellaneous coster carts. The four railways routes bring their swarms of folk; those who come to the stations in the town generally driving up in wagonettes, the coachmen attracting passengers by the familiar cry of "Bob a nob to the Downs."

The scene on the race-course has been described too often to require any full account here, and Frith's celebrated picture in the Tate Gallery, although old-fashioned, gives an excellent idea of the enormous assemblage.

One of the most remarkable features exists in the innumerable temporary wooden erections on the great slope opposite the Grand Stand. It is an enormous city of placarded booths everywhere blazing with colour. From Tattenham Corner there is always a good and comprehensive view of the scene without the unpleasantness of a crowd.

An old and very much respected tradesman of Epsom now holds the record of having seen the Derby run for more consecutive years than anyone living. Mr. Dearle, who is eighty-three years of age, is a tallow chandler, and carries on his business in a picturesque little shop in the High Street. He has now seen the famous race seventy-five times. In an interview published in a London daily paper he is represented to have said, "I believe I am the only man living now who has seen so many Derbies running. Old Joshua Aynes, a butcher of Walham Green, saw seventy-five Derby days, and when Lord Rosebery won with Ladas he sent him a five-pound note. But Aynes is dead now."

But of the Downs themselves nothing has yet been said. The spirit of them is so admirably rendered by Mr. Martin Tupper, that his lines may well be quoted here:—

The Downs.

"MY EPSOM RIDE.

" Pencilled in the saddle on a blank sheet of paper, May 28th, 1857, on going from Albury over the Downs to the Derby.

" The breezy downs and a spirited horse,
　And the honeyed breath of the golden gorse,
　And tinkling bells of the bleating ewes,
　And a bright panorama of changing views,
　And all that is peaceful and cheerful beside,
　Oh, these I get in my Epsom ride."

The "changing views" are very extensive, Epsom Downs being over 500 feet above sea level. To the north one looks across the town and the clay hills at Chessington, and beyond the Thames, right away to distant hills where the chalk passing beneath London, crops out at Wantage, St. Albans, and Hertford. Westwards the country is beautifully wooded, the foliage of Woodcote Park melting away imperceptibly towards Leatherhead and Cobham, and even Windsor Castle is visible in clear weather.

To the south are Walton Downs and the wooded heights of Headley, with the spire of its church cutting into the horizon. It is a beautiful view of steep hills embowered in trees, and is perhaps loveliest under a heavy cloud-laden sky, when great indigo lines of cumulus come rolling across the hills, blotting out all but the boldest features of the landscape. Banstead and the delicious valley near Nork Park are hidden from view by the larch coppices at Buckle's Gap.

CHAPTER VIII.

IN WHICH THE COUNTRY BEYOND THE DOWNS IS DESCRIBED.

FROM the upper windows of the houses of Epsom the view southwards is limited to the bare green ramparts of the Downs, broken only by the grand stand, the stunted Scotch firs and the larch plantations at Tattenham corner. Beyond is a view towards Walton-on-the-Hill and Headley, which is always a refreshing sight after the bleakness of the Downs, and never fails to receive the eulogies of journalists who come down for the races.

Looking south-west from near the grand stand, a hollow among the hills, known as Langley Bottom, runs along the margin of Woodcote Park. The Ermyn Street—a Roman road—takes one along one side of this valley, and by keeping to the left one is led up to a finger-post, where roads diverge in four directions. It is a good road only as far as the first turning to the right; beyond that point it is mainly rough and grassy, gradually becoming entirely grass-grown. Keeping a straight course, it seems to lose itself on Mickleham or Cherkley Down, and only debouches upon the main Dorking or Leatherhead road near Juniper Hall in the form of a rough water-worn path. No doubt the Ermyn Street joined itself with the Stane Street, which runs in a perfectly straight line through Ockley, formerly joining Horsham and Dorking. At the four ways before mentioned, the turning to the left as one approaches from Langley

Bottom leads to Headley—that to the right to Ashtead Park. The Headley road is quite open on the right, and the altitude of 370 feet at this point gives wide views over the steadily rising hills to the south, and down the valley to many miles of country beyond Ashtead in the opposite direction. Scarcely a quarter of a mile from the finger-post, a road branches off to the right, running across the open arable land like a biscuit-coloured ribbon, without hedge or ditch on either side, until it disappears between hedges just where the ground commences to rise nearly 200 feet to the village of Headley. The lane to the right passes a picturesque farmstead at the turning to Walton, but brings one to the same destination as that to the left. Although it entails a longer hill, this turning to the right is extremely pretty on account of its steep banks of ruddy-coloured soil, picturesquely overgrown with ivy, hollies, bracken and a hundred other woodland plants. Emerging from the deep portion of the lane, Mr. Walter Cunliffe's house, Headley Court, appears across an intervening depression. It is a stately, red brick, modern structure, with many tiled gables and well-designed chimneys; it is, indeed, of that class of sober red brick Tudor house which seems to belong to England's soil more than any other style. Headley Park, the residence of Mr. John Newton Mappin, stands on the left, but much nearer the road. In its present newness of aspect it is a little startling in its black and white half-timbered gable ends and its mixture of tiles, slate and red brick, with white paint on most of the woodwork (there is no disparagement of white paint intended); but the healing hand of time will doubtless subdue the various contrasting materials, and produce a harmony which does not exist at present.

After a bend in the road, an extremely picturesque and leafy little corner appears. Steep grassy banks, the village forge, and a great hoary elm on a triangular patch of green, are some of the chief features. Climbing still further between high shady banks of what is known as Oyster Hill, from the fossil oysters discovered there, the road reaches the highest point by the church

and the little cluster of cottages constituting the nucleus
of the village of Headley. The "Cock" Inn hangs out
a sign opposite the little shop where most necessities
can be bought from groceries to postal orders. Close to
the churchyard there is a tiny piece of water, and facing
one is the church tower, surmounted by its ponderous

Headley
Church. shingled spire, which is such a landmark
from Epsom Downs. The entire building,
designed by Mr. G. E. Street, and dedicated
to St. Mary, dates from 1853-4, when the old building
was pulled down. Its site is marked by a double
row of clipped yews (planted where the pillars stood),
a little to the south of the new church. The other
remains of the former building, consisting of odd
pieces of stone, are built into the form of a grotto over
the vault where lie the remains of the Rev. Ferdinand
Faithfull, a former rector. He was father of Emily
Faithfull, who was born at Headley Rectory, and died
in May, 1895. Her active interest in the condition of
working women led her to found a printing establishment, where women were employed as compositors.
Queen Victoria so approved of her work that she
appointed Miss Faithfull printer and publisher in ordinary
to Her Majesty.

Owing to the exposed position, the stone of
the new structure is weathering rapidly, although the
flint work retains its newness through the same cause.
The roofs are slate and the spire is shingled, but the
three lych gates, also modern, are covered with Horsham
slabs, and are quite an ornament to the graveyard.
Inside, the building seems chiefly remarkable for its
length, emphasised if one enters through the tower,
which stands at the west end of the aisleless nave. In
the chancel, recently wainscoted with oak, there is a
carved oak chair, presented by Mr. Walter Cunliffe, of
Headley Court, in 1893, and a painted triptych beneath
the east window to Charles Timberlake Harrison, dated
1895. The window at the east of the north wall of the
chancel is to the memory of the Hon. Mary Greville
Howard. "She was sometime patron of the living,
and a constant benefactor to the church and parish."

Her features are faithfully portrayed in the stained glass, with the word, " Caritas," and M.G.H., 1875. Representations of the new church and schools are shown in the upper corners. In the vestry there is a little mural monument of wood painted to represent black veined marble. In Manning and Bray's " History of Surrey" this is described as marble. The inscription runs :

> " Underneath lyeth ye body of Mrs. Elizabeth Leate, daughter of Mr. Nicholas Leat, Turkey Merchant, a worthy and eminent citizen of London, and of Joanna, daughter of Mr. Richard Stapers, alderman of that city, who, with many of their children, are interred in St. Martin Oteswich Church in London. She deceased ye 5th day of May, Anno Domini 1680, being aged 80 years. 'Though after my skin worms destroy this body, yet in my flesh shall I see God.' Job xix. 26. Her nephew, Richard Wyld, rector of this Church, with whom she lived the last six years of her life, placed this in memorial of her."

Several of the lancet windows are filled with stained glass, one in the south wall of the nave to George Lyall, of Headley, M.P. for Whitehaven and Governor of the Bank of England, who died in 1881 ; and another to Henry Cunliffe, who died at Homburg in 1883. The octagonal font is modern, the arch opening into the tower is richly moulded, and the oaken spiral staircase to the belfry is a fine piece of joinery. The clock strikes on a fifteenth century bell of Sussex casting. Close to the staircase is a small monument to Simon Crane, who died on August 20th, 1775, at the age of 75, when on a visit to Headley Court ; while another marble monument in the tower is to John Edwin, fifth and youngest son of Sir Humphrey Edwin, formerly Lord Mayor of London, who died on the 4th of May, 1753, aged 72.

The earliest church at Headley seems to have been built in the year 1317 ; the first entry in the register, however, is no earlier than 1663—the year, it is interesting to note, that Mary Stydolf became patroness of the living. This Mary was the wife of William Stydolf, Esquire of the Body to Charles I, who became lord of the manor in 1593. Aubrey gives some interesting details of the improvements to the church carried out by Mary Stydolf :

1. She seeled and beautifyed the church An. D. 1666, the yeare of the Great Plague, and caused a new light to be made to help the darkness of the church.
2. She beautifyed the chancel and gave 1 damask communion cloth. (This communion cloth is still preserved.)
. She gave a stone font with a fair wainscot cover.
4. She erected a canopy over the pulpit, and gave a cushion and covering for the pulpit of green cloath with a silk fringe.
5. She help'd the decayed Belfry of the Church and adorned it.

Whether the place should be spelt Headley or Hedley is open to much discussion, although the modern official acceptation is Headley. In the Domesday Book it is called Hallega, but that does not give much light upon the present form of the name. By the year 1314 it is given as Hedleigh, and in 1558 it is written Hedley, but it was written Headley as long ago as 1771.

The spelling of the name Headley.

A very interesting custom existed among the shepherds of Headley Downs during Aubrey's day—the latter part of the 17th century. In his "Antiquities of Surrey," speaking of Headley, he says :—"The Shepherds of these Downs use a half Horn, slitt *secundum Longitudinem,* nail'd to the end of a long staff, with which they can hurl a stone a great distance, and so keep the Sheep within their bounds, or from straggling into the corn." He adds : "But never saw the thing until I pass'd over these pleasant Downs." Brayley speaks of an enquiry made in 1808 about the custom, an old fellow then living having stated that he could remember when the shepherds of that part had a horn at one end of their crooks, in which they placed a small stone, and throwing it by that means could hit a sheep as far off as 20 rods. According to the old man, the custom had died out since about 1760.

Upon the breezy heath a little way beyond the church, one of those wide views offered at intervals from one end of the North Downs to the other, spreads itself out towards the west. One looks across the purple heather and bright green bracken to a horizon formed by the wooded heights above the valley of the Mole with the spire of Ranmore

Headley Heath.

HEADLEY HEATH.

The view looking westwards across the valley of the Mole, showing the spire of Ranmore Church on the horizon.

Church a conspicuous landmark.   From here as from
every other point of view this valley has the subtle
charm of closely timbered country, and there is further
contentment for those who regret the fate of Hindhead
in the absence of any new buildings.   Indeed the only
buildings in sight are The White House, a comfortable,
unpretentious, stuccoed house overlooking the heath,
and High Ashurst whose chimney stacks peep out from
the surrounding trees.   Southward a road crosses the
heath, leading to Box Hill if one keeps to the right
passing a gate into the woods crowning the Betchworth Hills.   From Betchworth Clump, a coppice
occupying one of the highest points, there is a wide and
interesting view towards the south, but the surface of
the country at one's feet is unpleasantly disturbed by
some quarries.   Turning towards Walton-on-the-Hill,

Pebble Hill. a bend in the road suddenly reveals a dark
green abyss down which a road has had the
audacity to climb.   To any but Alpine cyclists this
Pebble Hill is impossible for riding, to wheel a bicycle
down between the steep banks and overarching trees
being a sufficiently awkward undertaking.   Close to
the hill and hidden in summer by the dense foliage, is
Pebblecombe, a large modern house.   Avoiding Pebble
Hill, the lane leads past Frith Park and out on to Walton
Heath.   Across this plateau of light green bracken
and dark green gorse runs the main road to Banstead
and Sutton, with wide views on every side.   A turning
on the left leads into a less frequented road and brings
one into the village of Walton-on-the-Hill.

The church, with its red-capped tower overlooking

Walton-on-
the-Hill. the triangular patch of green, has such a
new external appearance that one would
never expect to find that it contained a
remarkable late Norman leaden font.   It consists of a
circular drum of cast lead, resting on a stone column.
A number of Norman arches occupied by saints in a
sitting posture, run round the leaden basin and give it
a very rich appearance.   There are traces of the hinge
and fastening of the wooden cover which has disappeared.   At Brookland, in Romney Marsh, there

is a similar font to this one with figures illustrating the months, and in the church of St. Evroult de Montfort, near Rouen, there is another, showing figures of the months and of the Zodiac. Altogether there are just

THE REMARKABLE LEADEN FONT OF THE LATE NORMAN PERIOD
IN WALTON-ON-THE-HILL CHURCH.

thirty of these leaden fonts in this country, all of them dating from about the end of the eleventh century.

In plan the church, which is dedicated to St. Peter, consists of a nave and chancel with a wide north aisle, separated by an arcade of two arches which was added in 1870. The tower at the west end of the nave containing a small gallery took the place of an old wooden one, probably similar to that of Great Bookham, about the year 1820. Of this new tower, however, only the lower portion remains, for in 1896 the upper part, built in three stages and ornamented with pinnacles, came down to make way for a more simple style. The nave was rebuilt at the expense of the parish about the year 1820, so that the chancel is now the only portion of the 13th century church remaining. Although restored, it fortunately preserves on the outside of the north wall the recessed tomb of the founder, John de Walton.

The oak screen was placed between the nave and chancel by Mrs. Tanqueray in 1887 in memory of her husband. Twenty or more odd pieces of painted glass are preserved in a window in the south wall of the nave. Facing the font is a chained Bible, dated 1803, upon a reading desk which is of modern construction, and, although one or two pieces of the carved oak upon it are old, they have been placed in the church comparatively recently. The chain was brought from Salisbury Cathedral, where it had for several years been used for a similar purpose.

Both the green outside the church and the village street are green and shady, but one would willingly see fewer broken down walls and unkempt gardens, for these things detract much from the charm of an otherwise perfectly situated village.

Walton Place stands near the church. It is an ancient and an interesting house, having very solid walls as well as fine chimney stacks and buttresses. Anne of Cleves lived here after her separation from Henry the Eighth, and Brayley states that prior to 1785 the building contained a chapel, having a stone pulpit. This was the chapel of the Monastery which formerly stood here. The chapel exists to-day, but it has been divided into two floors, and so modernised that one can scarcely recognise the monastic building.

At the time of the Norman invasion Walton-on-the-Hill was simply Waltone, the last three words being more or less modern to distinguish it from

Walton-on-Thames and Walton-on-the-Naze.   Salmon
in his antiquities of Surrey (1736), says, " I believe
it owes its name to that earth-work which is seen on
the Downs above Mickleham, pointing one way towards

ON WALTON HEATH.
From the Reigate Road, looking westwards.

Lethered, the other towards Walton by the end of
Pebble Lane.   This seems to have been a British or
Saxon Limit for division of the country, and probably
runs through some part of Walton which may be
defaced with ploughing."

But before even Saxon times Walton must have been inhabited, for the Roman remains discovered on the heath have been considerable. In 1772 some foundations and walls, a portion of a flue constructed chiefly of bricks and flat tiles, and a small brass figure of Esculapius were discovered and reported to the Society of Antiquaries. Within a large enclosure of earthwork, what was supposed to have been the prætorium of a Roman station was discovered in 1808. Fragments of pottery and other remains were dug out, and about half a mile to the west a well, fifteen feet in circumference, was unearthed. The lower portion was thought to have fallen in, for there was no water in it, and it was probably very much deeper when in use by the Romans of this station, for the wells of the district are upwards of three hundred feet in depth.

Roman Remains at Walton-on-the-Hill.

Toland described Walton and Headley as "both too windy, too woody, and therefore in summer too close," but he also mentions that many woods were being felled, so that the objection was not likely to continue long. Headley is woody still, but it is never close in summer, and Walton verges more towards bleakness than the other extreme. The extensive and wind-swept heath is exceptionally beautiful when the heather is in bloom, and the view southwards extends from beyond Reigate to Box Hill. Dominating the ridge there still stands a windmill which adds much to the picturesqueness of these downs. There was a mill at Walton-on-the-Hill in the reign of Edward I, and the present one possibly stands on the site of its predecessor, built about six hundred years ago.

Tadworth Court, near the junction of the Dorking and Reigate roads, was the home of Lord Russell of Killowen, Lord Chief Justice of England. He died here on August 10th, 1900, and is buried in the southern portion of Epsom Cemetery.

If one passes along the high road towards Reigate the modern church of Kingswood is passed among the trees on the left, the stone spire being visible from all over the heath. Kingswood

Kingswood.

Warren, the seat of Mr. Cosmo Bonsor, M.P., is
hidden by the trees a little to the west.   About a half
a mile beyond the church a turning on the same side
leads through a valley chiefly occupied with plough

Chipstead
Church.

lands to the out-of-the-way little green by
Chipstead Church. The green, always quiet
and reposeful, is never dusty even late in the
summer, for there is too little traffic to disturb the
surface of the road.   Not only is the green surrounded by
fine trees but the lanes leading up to it and the churchyard itself are full of fine timber.   The pretty lych
gate, the dark yew tree, and the perfect little cruciform
building form an ideal picture of the old English church.
In the steeply sloping graveyard

> " The very graves appeared to smile,
> So fresh they rose in shadow'd swells."

And the views of the green hills towards the east are
seen through a framework of elm leaves.   The central
tower of the church, which is dedicated to St. Margaret,
is heavy and low.   It bears the date 1631 on the west
side of its parapet, although the greater part of both
tower and chancel date from about the year 1132.
The nave is Norman, being divided from the aisles by
arcades of pointed arches resting on circular pillars.
Small lancet windows light the building so that the
interior is generally dim to emphasising the height of
the massive stone vaulting which supports the tower.
Across the chancel runs an old oak screen, bearing the
royal arms, where in former times the rood was placed.
From the south side of the chancel is suspended a
tattered banner beneath a helmet surmounted by the
crest of the Stephens family of Epsom, to whom there are
some memorial slabs in the floor.   On the opposite side
of the chancel there is a piscina, and in the north wall
of the north transept are two aumries, one of them
fitted with a shelf.   Another aumry is in the south
transept.   The font has an octagonal basin decorated
with flamboyant tracery, supported on a thick circular
base.   The six-sided carved oak pulpit and the reading
desk are Jacobean.   On the south side of the nave there
are three little blocked up clerestory windows.

CHIPSTEAD CHURCH,

A Norman Cruciform Building.

The most interesting memorial in the church is to the memory of Sir Edward Banks, the builder of three of the most important bridges across the Thames, Waterloo, London and Southwark. In the centre of the monument, which is placed on the right as one enters by the porch, there is a bust of the bridge builder resting on a representation of an arch of London Bridge, while to the right and left appear arches of Southwark and Waterloo Bridges. The long inscription describes how Sir Edward Banks rose from the humblest ranks of life, having been blest by providence with "an honest heart, a clear head and an extraordinary degree of perseverance." He started as a common labourer, but raised himself to considerable wealth and a superior station in life. He first became known at Chipstead as a workman on the railway to Merstham, and having been attracted by the charming situation of the church he desired that his ashes might be conveyed there after his death. In addition to the bridges already mentioned the inscription on the monument refers to the naval works at Sheerness dockyard, and the new channels for the Ouse, Nen and Witham as the work of Sir Edward Banks.

Sir Edward Banks.

Just outside the porch near the wall of the south aisle is a flat stone tomb much overgrown with grass but showing traces of a decorated cross carved upon its surface. The fine old yew tree appearing in the view of the church given here is of great age and immense girth.

At the eastern end of the graveyard on a long wooden inscription board is the rather unusual verse

> " I was in the blooming of my years•
> I left my friends in floods of tears,
> And left a toilsome world behind
> A crown of glory for to find."

It is quite possible that Chipstead was a market town in Saxon times, for although the Normans wrote it Tepestede in their great survey, the earliest form of writing the name was Chepestede or Cepestede. Salmon says that *chepe* signifies a market, and "to barter for a thing is to *cheapen* it with us. We have Cheapside, Eastcheap, Chipping Wicomb, Chipping Norton,

Chipping Ongar." The Domesday book details two manors at Chipstead, one held by William de Watevile from the Abbey of Chertsey, and the other, the larger of the two, by Richard de Tonbrige. In 1736 a Mr. Docminique was Lord of the Manor.

The road leading towards Epsom is flanked and over-shadowed by huge beeches and elms—the crossroads near Shabden Park being beautifully wooded. In the late autumn these unfrequented lanes at Chipstead bring one in touch with those ideal golden autumns so constantly depicted at the Royal Academy Exhibitions.

Shabden Park, where Mr. Wentworth H. A. E. Cattley lives, stands close to the road. It is a modern house with a steep tiled roof and stone walls picturesquely hidden by creepers. From the house and from the roadway there

THE WELL HOUSE AT BANSTEAD.

are views over the wooded valley in which Kingswood lies. The cottages on the right as one approaches the village were built in 1871, although at a first glance they might be taken to be two centuries old. A little further on there is a roadside pond over-hung by trees, with some fine old barns appearing a little way off "hull down" as it were over the slope of the hill. Beyond the pond the road forks by the "White Hart Inn," which is not pretty in itself but is surrounded with over-arching elms. On a hot summer's morning this is a cool spot where one may look out between the trees on to the glaring yellow sunshine.

From Chipstead there are two ways of reaching **Banstead.** Banstead through pretty upland country. The interests of the village centre in the church, for the average cottage is commonplace, and beyond the curious little well-house on its patch of grass by the roadside, and the "Woolpack Inn," with its lovely old garden, there is little to attract attention, unless it be a peep of a fine old red brick house over high walls or hedges. All Saints—the parish church—has flint walls, the tower stands at the west end, and is surmounted by a sharp shingled spire, which is slightly out of perpendicular. There are nave, chancel, and two aisles extending on each side of the chancel in the form of chapels. After one is accustomed to the dim light of the interior, it becomes apparent that the walls are covered with stencilling and texts. The aisles are divided from the nave by arcades of pointed arches. The arch adjoining the chancel is lower than the remainder and has been cut into in a remarkable fashion, and a pillar on the south side of the chancel has its base sunk below the level of the floor just by a modern oak screen cutting off the south chapel.

In the vestry there is a fine old oak cabinet with richly carved panels. The font is octagonal on a circular base—when Brayley wrote it was painted in imitation of grey marble. Monuments to the Lambert family are numerous. Among them are those to Sir Daniel Lambert, Knight, Lord Mayor in 1741, Dame Mary Lambert his wife, and William Lambert, the last being a tablet sculptured by Legrew. In Garratt's Hall Chapel there is a brass not mentioned by Aubrey or Manning. It says, "Here lyeth ye body (of) Thomas Lambert Gent yeoman of ye (privy) chamber (vnto their Matis. King James and King Charles (the first).

> The da . . . .
> Being the . . . .
> . . . of . . . .
> . . that . . . .

Another memorial has this inscription : "Here lyeth interred ye body of Ruth Brett, the late wife of George Brett, citizen and goldsmith of London ; and daughter of Mr. Edward Lambert of this parish. She departed

BANSTEAD CHURCH FROM THE WEST.

this lyfe the sixth day of November Ao.D. 1647." Then follows a panegyric commencing :

"Behold the mirrour of her sex and kind,
Nature adorn'd her frame, virtue her mind.'

In addition to these there are tablets to the Motteux and Parry families, to Sir Edward Howarth, to Henry Leigh Spencer, to Major General Daniel Burr, and to the Wilmots and the Fryes.

The registers of Banstead are nearly perfect from the year 1547. They have been published by the Parish Register Society. Two porches, one opening into the north and one into the south aisle are attractive features of the exterior, so also are the dormer windows in the great red roof of the nave.

Banstead Downs are as breezy and as bare as those of Epsom ; they were, indeed, continuous in the 17th century. On July 14th, 1667, Pepys writes, " I walked upon the Downes, where a flock of sheep was ; and the most pleasant and innocent sight that ever I saw in my life. We found a shepherd and his little boy reading, far from any houses or sight of people, the Bible to him : and we took notice of his wooling knit stockings, of two colours mixed."

In addition to Banstead Church, there was one at Berghes or Burgh—the present day Burgh Heath—and another at St. Leonard's. They have both disappeared, but traces of St. Leonard's Chapel may be seen in the wood of that name situated on the south-west side of Burgh Heath. Up to about ten years ago the building spoken of by Salmon was still standing. He wrote, " There stands now by Mr. Buckle's house (Nork Park) a church or chapel reduced to a barn. This or that at *Preston* has been, I believe, a Parish Church once in the manor of Ewell." Unfortunately the barn has been pulled down.

Burgh Heath is on the dusty main road between Sutton and Reigate, its little collection of cottages and shops being of little interest, although the heath joining that of Walton without any perceptible break is on the whole a pretty spot. North-westward runs the road to Epsom, which, crossing the Downs, eventually becomes Church Street. Before it reaches Epsom Downs, it passes Nork Park, the seat of Mr. F. E. Colman. The house is closely surrounded by trees except on the north side, where it has a very wide view right across the valley of the Thames. Christopher Buckle built the house some time previous to his death in 1759. His grandson, another Christopher Buckle, sold the property in 1812 to the Rt. Hon. Charles George Percival, 2nd Baron Arden, whose widow continued to reside at Nork Park after his death.

The road to Walton-on-the-Hill, which passes close to Tattenham Corner, is not so rural now as formerly through the unhealed scar of the branch line of the South Eastern and Chatham stretching across the green hills. A handful of new houses have been placed by one of the stupendous embankments of chalky soil. The embankments and cuttings will soon become part of the surrounding country and from most points of view invisible, but the group of houses are a menace to the charm of this strip of country. One can merely trust that this hitherto unattacked piece of Surrey will be saved from the hands of the builder.

CHAPTER IX.

A DESCRIPTION OF THE COUNTRY
WEST OF THE TOWN.

A LONG the whole of the western side of Epsom
the Common is spread over a delightful strip of
upland country, wooded where it adjoins
Woodcote Park, and elsewhere covered with
gorse, bracken and brambles. The Dorking Road
crosses the centre of this breezy waste
land, and then plunges precipitously down-
wards towards Ashtead. It is a pretty
view from the top of the hill, with the white road
running away from one's feet and disappearing at a
bend among the trees below. Above and beyond the
dark masses of foliage in Ashtead Park there also
appears a distant blue horizon formed by the downs
above Dorking, and stretching from Ranmore Common
up the beautiful valley of the Mole towards Leatherhead. Parallel with the Dorking Road run the united
South Western and London and Brighton lines, severing
the Common with a cutting and an embankment. There
is, however, a road bridge leading up towards "The
Wells," the residence whose grounds hold the old wells.
A windmill formerly stood near the lodge of the house,
and old inhabitants of Epsom still remember it, but it
was unfortunately destroyed by fire on an "Oaks" day
many years ago. From this part of the Common one
looks down towards Christ Church and the cottages and
pond of Stamford Green. The smallest of this little collection of dwellings is little more than a wooden cabin. Round

Epsom Common.

about the pond it is quietly picturesque, and the flock of
white geese do their best to brighten the little green.
From the pond the deep blue-green gorse of the Common
forms the horizon to the west, but northwards the
wooded acres of Horton Manor are marred by the
tower of the new Asylum.

The road by the pond leads into West Hill in one
direction, and the other way passing Christ Church
brings one to a portion of the Common nearly two
hundred and fifty feet above sea level, with views over
a delightful forest-like stretch of country. Right away
to the left are the heavily-timbered undulations of
Ashtead and Woodcote Parks, imperceptibly running
off into the woods at the limits of the Common, and
continued in the Ashtead Woods, Pachesham Park and
Telegraph Hill, while against the blue horizon appears
the outline of Oxshott's beautiful and desolate common.

Half-a-mile further on, having passed on the left
some pieces of water known as the " Stew Ponds," the
road leaves the Common and runs between the hedges
of Rushet Lane until it enters at right angles the
Kingston and Leatherhead turnpike road, with a rough
grassy lane on the opposite side, still leading westward
and emerging near Cobham and Stoke D'Abernon
Station—three-quarters of a mile from Oxshott.
Another and more convenient way to reach the village
is by keeping to the main road, passing a small pottery
on the right and a very quaint little inn, " The
Fox and Hounds," on the left. Wide belts of grass
on either side dotted with furze bushes give the road
an interesting appearance, but it is a popular route
for the dust-raising and scorching cyclist, and should be
avoided on Saturday afternoons. After two miles there
appears on the right a gate and direction post to Stoke
D'Abernon and Oxshott. It is a right of way cutting
through a triangular piece of land between this and the
lane to Esher from Leatherhead. A little way inside
the gate there is a signally interesting view up the
valley of the Mole, with the wild country on the Downs
by Mickleham and Headley very conspicuous. Passing
through the gate at the other end of this short cut and

THE DORKING ROAD

Where it crosses Epsom Common, looking towards Ashtead.

turning to the right, the village of Oxshott lies just a
mile to the north-west. The usual centre
of interest is missing here, for Oxshott has
no church, and it is doubtless for this
reason that Surrey historians completely ignore the
place; even Murray's latest edition merely mentions the
railway station. But although the church is missing,
there is undoubtedly a village here with two inns. The
" Queen Victoria " has been renovated or rebuilt and

Oxshott
Village.

IN OXSHOTT VILLAGE.

is not of any interest, while the " Bear " is a quaint
little place with a pretty view from its windows, for
Oxshott, be it remembered, is an upland hamlet. The
triangular little green is a pleasant spot, with big trees
and a fine farm as the prominent features. An iron
building—the Parochial School overlooking the Green
—is used for a service in connection with Stoke
D'Abernon on Sunday evenings, but it is possible that
this will be replaced by a more permanent building.

Of Stoke D'Abernon and its interesting church,
and of the other villages and manorial seats in the

neighbourhood of Leatherhead, this book does not propose to treat.

The prettiest route to Ashtead is by way of Woodcote Green, up the hill on to the Common, and then by the road skirting Woodcote Park. Just before leaving the Common a fair-sized piece of water known as Baron's Pond lies on the right side of the road. It is a secluded spot, surrounded by bushes and sedgy ground, and the sunsets reproduced on the surface of the water are often of the loveliest. The pond received its name from Baron De Teissier who formerly resided at Woodcote Park.

Half-a-mile from the pond there is a yawning chalk pit, with the road to Headley winding up one side of it, while that to Ashtead starts off in much the same direction but immediately alters its mind, swinging sharply round and leading straight up to the gates of Ashtead Park. A cottage just inside this entrance bears over its doorway a sundial dated 1734. The public may use the main avenue through the grounds,

Ashtead Park. but are of course obliged to keep to it strictly. From the road the views extend across the grassy slopes, dotted with splendidly grown oaks, walnuts, elms and Spanish chestnuts, to the house—a comparatively modern building of white brick and stone. It is built in the form of a large square, with a portico and a wide terrace on the north side. From this terrace there is a delightful view over the park—about 140 acres in extent—the ground gradually falling away towards the lake. A fine herd of deer is generally to be seen grazing in the shade of the trees.

John Evelyn in his diary, under the date Dec. 30th, 1665, writes: "To Woodcott, where I supp'd at my Lady Mordaunt's at Ashted, where was a room hung with *Pintado*, full of figures great and small, prettily representing sundry trades and occupations of the Indians, with their habits; here supp'd also Dr. Duke, a learned and facetious gentleman."

Again on the 10th of May, 1684: "I went to visit my brother *(Richard Evelyn at Woodcote)* in Surrey.

Call'd by the way at Ashted, where Sir Robert Howard (Auditor to the Exchequer) entertain'd me very civilly at his new built house, which stands in a Park on the Downe, the avenue South; tho' downe hill to the house, which is not greate, but with the outhouses very convenient. The staire-case is painted by Verrio with the storie of Astrea; amongst other figures is the picture of the Painter himselfe, and not unlike him; the rest is well done, onely the columns did not at all please me; there is also Sir Robert's own Picture in an oval; the whole in *fresca*. The place has this great defect, that there is no water but what is drawn up by horses from a very deep well."

Sir Robert Howard, the sixth son of Thomas, first Earl of Berkshire, had purchased the Ashtead Estate from Henry, Duke of Norfolk, grandson of the Earl of Arundel, in 1680—four years before the visit paid by Evelyn just mentioned. The house standing at that time was described by Aubrey in his "Natural History of Surrey," as "an handsome seat, with a neat garden very pleasantly situated," but Sir Robert Howard pulled this down and erected in its place the mansion with the "staire-case . . . painted by Verrio." Sir Robert was, besides being a historian and dramatist, a famous man of his age, and is said to have received visits at this house from Charles II, James II, and William III.

The present house took the place of Sir Robert's one nearly a hundred years ago, and is now the seat of Mr. Pantia Ralli.

One of the most charming features of the Park next to its splendid timber is a fine old brick wall, surrounding it. The bricks are a lovely subdued red, tinted with delicate grey-green or bright yellow lichen, while here and there the top of the wall is covered with moss, or entirely overgrown with small-leaved ivy, and where it runs along the Dorking Road it is heavily buttressed.

Near the lodge gates on the road just mentioned there are some fine cedars, and between the house itself and the Church is an avenue of limes of considerable age and beauty.

The Church, dedicated to St. Giles, is so hidden by
the trees of the Park that it is not easy for
a stranger to find, especially as the gates
of the approach are similar to those of the
Park, and do not in any way suggest the proximity of
a church.   Passing up the avenue, the very solid
battlemented and spireless tower comes into view.   Its
walls are of a yellowish plaster with stone dressings,
and traces of red brickwork appearing in places, giving
the building a welcome touch of colour.   The roofs
are entirely covered with Horsham slabs, and the
other walls are of open flint work.   A fine old yew
occupies a prominent position by the tower, and all
round the grave-yard there are splendid trees, where
rooks and jackdaws squabble and caw from early dawn.

Ashtead
Church.

ASHTEAD CHURCH.

It stands on the site of a Roman Camp.

Wood-pigeons, too, are plentiful, and if one is quietly hidden for a time scores of rabbits will come out and feed at the head of the avenue.

By a winding stone staircase in the corner turret of the tower the roof may be reached, and the climb is worth the trouble if the day be fine, for there is an unusually rich sylvan view above the tree tops. The eight bells were cast in 1873. The Church itself consists of a nave, a chancel, a north transept of considerable size and a north chapel, the roofs of each being very beautiful. The panelling is of Havannah cedar, while the arches rest on carved wooden figures of angels— standing, and each holding a scroll of parchment. All the pews, formerly of Australian cedar, were exchanged for oak in 1891 ; the pulpit—a modern one—is of finely carved oak ; the font—"ancient" according to Brayley —is hexagonal, with the basin carved with quatrefoils on the sides, and a little lower down with grotesque grinning heads alternated with plain shields.

Over the altar, which was brought from Woodcote Park, is a carved stone reredos, with its niches filled with carved alabaster figures.

In the vestry is a fine old chair with a narrow carved back, similar to one formerly standing by the altar, also an ancient plan of the parish, and a list of the rectors and vicars from Robert de Montfort, who was instituted before 1282.

A small room opening out of the north transept in which the untidy odds and ends of the Church are kept, has also a corner cupboard of very dark wood standing upon twisted wooden legs. The wood seems to be oak, and its age must be very considerable.

The **Monuments.** On the floor of the chancel there are some ancient brasses. One of them reads :

"Vnder this Stone lies Elizabeth, berefte of mortall lyfe,
  Christ's faithfull seruaunt Fromond's child & Bodleis louing wyfe.
        Died the 2 of March, anno Dni 1591."

This Elizabeth was probably a daughter of one of the Fromonds whose monuments may be seen in the Lumley Chapel at Cheam. Close to this, and also on the floor, is another brass, easily decipherable :

> " Here lyeth bvryed the bodye of John Browne
>   Esqvier late Sergeant of Her Maiesties Wood
>   Yeard and Edith his late wife wch Edith deceased
>   T . . . . day of July 1590."

Another brass on the north wall of the chancel is to Dorothea Quinnella, dated 1640.

On the north wall of the nave is a marble monument to Lady Diana Fielding, whose bust of white marble is enclosed by a circle of darker stone below a pediment, with the arms of Howard and Warren above. The north wall of the chancel has a richly carved memorial to Sarah, relict of Nicholas Bond, of Earth, in the county of Cornwall. She was notable for her devotion to the poor of Ashtead, for whose benefit she left £500 at her death in 1712. The monument is ornamented with cupids, flowers, and a vase from which issue gilded flames. There are several monuments to members of the Howard family and others of lesser interest.

The east window, showing a representation of the Crucifixion in the centre, is believed to be by Lambert Lombard, of Liége, the master of Franz Floris ("the Flemish Raphael"). It came from the Abbey of Herckenrode, when it was dismantled in 1801, and was obtained for Mrs. Howard, of Ashtead Park, by Sir Charles Bagot, Ambassador at The Hague.

Among the tombs in the graveyard there are four, side by side, richly ornamented with skulls and other gruesome designs.

In Anglo-Saxon times Ashtead was known as *Stede*, and in the Domesday Book it is referred to by that name, while the Church stands upon a piece of ground once entirely surrounded by a deep trench, still visible in places. Brayley thinks that it probably formed the enceinte of some Roman villa or castramentation. Roman tiles are undoubtedly built into the arch of a window on the north side. It is now closed up. During the restoration some sixty years ago pieces of a Roman hypocaust were discovered. One piece has a slightly raised outline of a wolf attacking a stag, and the letters G. I. S. G. and I. W. E. The lower edge shows that the design was repeated.

The Roman remains.

The village of Ashtead is not remarkable for any thing in particular. It lies on a gentle slope on the road between Epsom and Leatherhead, and has at the bottom of the hill an inn whose quaintness lies chiefly in its name, "Ye Legge of Muttone and ye Cauliflowere." There are signs of the old building at the back, but the front view is now all new red brick, replacing some very picturesque wooden walls. Another inn on the other side of the road higher up the hill towards Epsom was known as "The Haunch of Venison." The building is still standing, but it is now converted into a very quiet-looking, comfortable private house. On the Leatherhead side there are some new buildings in which photographic materials are manufactured.

The railway station, served by the South Western and Brighton lines lies north of the village, just beyond the wide green with its scattered cottages. At this corner of Ashtead there are quite a number of new houses, tending to give a slightly suburban appearance, but the design of most of them is good.

North of the railway Ashtead Common runs off into the woods, so favoured by school treats in the summer. Most of the trees are oaks and there is little under-growth, but in spring and autumn these woods are very pleasant. An entrenchment, probably of Roman origin, lies hidden among the trees. It encloses nearly three acres of ground, and is about four hundred and twenty yards in circumference. A well of similar nature to that upon Epsom Common may also be found in the forest after some searching.

Where the drinking fountain, presented by the Hon. Mrs. Howard, now stands—opposite the almshouses— the stocks, whipping post, and pound were formerly situated. Their position is fast being forgotten, only a very few old folk remembering them before they were removed.

CHAPTER X.

THE ANCIENT PALACE OF NONSUCH, AND THE COUNTRY NORTH OF THE TOWN.

SCARCELY more than a mile from Epsom in the direction of London lies Ewell—picturesque, irregular, and showing traces of having been of more importance in other days.

The main street is still quaint and interesting, with little or nothing to jar with its charming old-world shops and cottages. One group is conspicuously attractive, with its low tiled roof, its over-hanging upper storey and its plastered walls, pierced with very little windows. In front of two or three of the shops are some pollard limes, so close that their branches almost touch the walls. These trees were most likely planted when Epsom had lined its High Street with limes and elms. Near the gates of Garbrand Hall, where the Kingston Road joins the main road from London, there was formerly a small butcher's shop, but it had been pulled down to widen the roadway before Brayley's History of Surrey was written (1845). The original market house is believed to have been built about 1570; it stood at the junction of Church Street with the High Street, in the centre of the open space which was larger than it is now, the houses on one side having since encroached upon it.

It was doubtless the centre of busy scenes many years

Ewell Village.

The Market House.

K

EWELL, HIGH STREET,
Showing the corner of Church Street on the right.

ago, for Ewell was not only a sufficiently important place to be head of a Deanery, but up to the middle of the seventeenth century a weekly market was regularly held, although the date of its origin is unknown. Annual sheep and cattle fairs, famous enough to bring together sheep breeders from all over the kingdom, took place on the 12th of May and the 29th of October. To-day the markets are held at Epsom, but a field adjoining the

THE WATCH-HOUSE IN CHURCH STREET, EWELL

"Green Man" inn and the Reigate Road is still pointed out where the annual fair was held.

Near the opposite corner of Church Street the quaint little watch-house may still be seen, its stucco-covered wall pierced by two doorways, and an opening above filled with iron bars. Here the disorderly folk of the village were

The Watch House.

locked up over night, being taken on to Epsom the
next morning.   An old and highly respected inhabitant
of Ewell clearly remembers, when a boy, seeing ne'er-
do-weels confined in the little house.   He also recalls
how it was no one's concern to watch the prisoners,
whose chums he has actually seen passing pewter pots
of ale and long churchwarden clay pipes through the
grating still remaining in one of the solid oak doors.
But the advent of the metropolitan police has removed
such proceedings to the picturesque days of beadles
and stocks, and now the watch-house only shelters a
useful little fire engine.

Ewell stands on a spot where the chalk of the Downs
joins the clay districts to the north-east. At the junction
of the two strata rise a number of springs of pure water,
forming the head of the pretty little stream known as
the Hogsmill River, which, flowing through rich
meadows at Old Malden, joins the Thames at Kingston.
These springs forming a fair-sized piece of water at the
commencement of the Kingston Road, not only give
their name to the old " Spring Hotel," but there seems
little doubt that they also gave Ewell its name, the
accepted derivation of the Domesday rendering
Ætwelle, or Etwel, being a corruption of At ye well.

Out of the main street of the village run two or
three lanes, flanked with high red brick walls, relieved
by cottages, chiefly old and picturesque.   Quite a
number of these are covered with that form of tile
which, when in place, has the appearance of brickwork.
They were extensively manufactured here at the time of
the brick tax, when so many subterfuges were resorted
to for evading it.   In two directions the limits of
the place are more or less proscribed by its position in
the narrowing angle formed by the two lines of railway
meeting at Epsom, but Ewell fortunately does not
evince any great symptoms of expansion, and both
stations are so far just beyond the reach of houses of
any sort.   The South Western Station is, during the
greater part of the summer, a wonderful rose garden,
individual bushes being often one blaze of red roses,
seemingly indifferent to the smoke of the engines.

THE TOWER AND GRAVEYARD OF EWELL OLD CHURCH.

From near the platforms, too, there are views of the village
as typically lovely as may be imagined, for in the
meadows down by the stream there grow huge elms,
and between these, backed by the distant foliage of
Nonsuch Park, appear the simple little pinnacled tower
of the modern church (the " modern " has no stigma in
this case) with the ivy-draped tower of the former
building beyond, and clustered among tall evergreen
shrubs, the red roofs of the village.   A large flour mill,
whose tall chimney is not conspicuous on account of
the neighbouring elms, stands on the stream.   That it
has been there for a considerable time may be easily
guessed from the ancient appearance of one side of the
mill, and it is not unlikely that a mill has been there
from the middle ages—it may even stand on the site of
one of those two mills mentioned in the Domesday
Survey, and valued at 10s.

The new Church, in Early English style, stands right
on the main road, while the hoary tower of
the old one is modestly in the background,
and is probably never noticed by the
swarms of Londoners who race past it on bicycles on
fine Saturdays and Sundays throughout the summer.
In 1848 the old Church of St. Mary was pulled down
with the exception of the tower—used as a chapel during
burial services until two years ago—and the present
Church was built at the same time by the Rev. Sir
George Glyn. The old structure was of the Perpendicular
style, and had a nave, a chancel, and a south aisle,
with a chapel opening from it. The tower is smothered
in ivy to such an extent that the walls are scarcely
visible.   They are of flint, faced with very worn
stone, and in the upper portion there are several
courses of red brick.   Most of the brasses and monuments were taken to the new church at the re-building,
but the old grave-yard, moist and shady from the tall trees
surrounding it, has a large collection of old head stones,
one of them, on the south-west side, being specially
noticeable for the medallion portrait in bold relief of
Jane Challoner, who lies buried beneath. To the north-
west of the tower a plain stone records the following :—

Ewell
Church.

"Catherine, wife of James Bailey, who in consequence of the overturning of the Dorking Coach, April, 1826, met with her death in the 22nd year of her age."

The accident occurred just by the old watch-house at the corner of Church Street. The coach had been pulled up in Church Street and the driver had got down, leaving a boy in charge of the horses. Something frightened the animals, for they started off suddenly, and the coach overturned as it was coming sharply into the main street of the village. It may be wondered why the driver should have driven down Church Street instead of going straight along the main road. This is easily explained from the fact that the lane running past the old church and turning at right angles into Church Street in front of Ewell Castle, *was* the main road in 1826, and it was only on account of the awkwardness and danger of the old route that the road was diverted to its present course. For some time the new thoroughfare went through the shallow pond forming the head of the Hogsmill River, but the inconvenience of this led to the water being carried in pipes under a properly constructed surface. The proximity of a headstone in the churchyard inscribed to a Weller, to the one connected with the coach disaster, and the neighbouring inn at Epsom, "The Marquis of Granby," have such a flavour of the Pickwick Papers that one cannot help wondering whether Dickens ever explored Ewell Churchyard and Epsom just afterwards.

Red-tiled roofs above white stone-work give the new church an attractive appearance. It is a large building with chancel, nave, south aisle, and a north aisle as wide as the nave.

The organ chamber was added at the restoration in 1893, and the pulpit, an elaborate one of alabaster and various marbles, was given in memory of the son and daughter of Edward W. and Jessie Martin in 1897. The font, believed to be Tudor, and the communion table came out of the old church. In the chancel, divided from the nave by a dark oaken screen, also brought from the former church, there are six monuments all fixed to the south wall. The largest and most

imposing of these is to the memory of Sir William
Lewen, Lord Mayor of London in 1717, who died in
1721. He is presented in marble, after the fashion of
his time in a huge wig and Lord Mayor's robes. The
other monuments in the chancel are to Col. Thomas
Glyn, late of His Majesty's 1st regiment of foot-guards,
Sir Richard, Jane, Lady Glyn and Sir George Glyn.
There are in addition four modern brasses to the Glyn
family, one of them on the north wall to the Rev. Sir
George Lewen Glyn, vicar of the parish of Ewell
for fifty years, from 1831 to 1881. The large Prayer
Book still in use is dated 1735 (George II), and has
a frontispiece showing St. Paul's Cathedral. The
reredos was given by Sir Gervas Glyn in 1893.

But it is in the collection of brasses in the south
aisle that the chief interest of the Church is concentrated, although the lettering is in most cases extremely
difficult to read. The earliest is dated 1510, and runs:

"Of your charite, pray for the Soule of Edmond Dows, gentil-
man, oon of the Clerks of the Signett with Kyng Harry the VII
whiche decessed the xiiij day of May, the yere of our Lord God
MCCCCC and X on whose soule Jhu have mercy. Amen."

Underneath another brass plate to the Hords is a man
in a gown and a woman praying; on one side of the man
are three sons kneeling, with these names over them:

Arther H——   Alyn H——   Edmund H——

Behind the woman are three daughters kneeling, named

Dorothe H——   Elizabeth H ——   Anne H——

The inscription of the brass to the Lady Dorothe
Taylare, runs:

" Here lyeth the Lady Dorothe Taylare, Widow, and Edmonde
Horde her seconde sonne; the which Edmond deceased the 29
day of October Ao. 1575, and she being the dawghter of Thomas
Roberde of Wylesdon in Mydellsexe, Esquyre, late the wyffe of
Syr Lawrence Taylàre of Doddington in the countye of Hunting-
ton, Knyght; & before wyffe unto Allen Horde of ye Myddle
Temple, Esquire; & Bencher there, ye yeres of her age was
LXX & deceased ye XIth of Maye Ao. 1577."

Above are brasses to the five sons and five daughters
of the Horde family on either side of the figure of a
woman.

Another brass reads very quaintly :

"Pray for me Lady Jane Iwarby sumtyme wife of Sr. John Iwarby of Ewell Knyght, daught' of John Agmondesham sumtyme of Ledered in Surrey Squier which Jane dyed the viii day of May in ye yere of Oure Lord MVcXIX of home Jhesu have mercy."

Close to this a praying female figure in brass says, "Lady help me and you."

A grave in the chancel of the old church marked the burying place of Sir Richard Bulkeley, a gentleman of large estates in Ireland, who died in 1710 at the age of 47.

The earliest entry in the Register of Ewell parish is in the year 1604.

Aubrey quotes a strange story from John Taylor the water poet. It was printed in London in 1630, and was entitled, "A murther committed by John Rowse on two of his children." This man Rowse lived at Ewell and fell into a vicious way of living, which caused his good wife to die of a broken heart. He married again and had two children, both girls, but owing to his disgraceful living he lost most of his income, and left for London in company with his servant maid. After continuing his evil course, and being robbed of the remainder of his property by a false friend, Rowse returned from the Low Countries to his home at Ewell, and was well received by his wife and children. But fearing that his little girls might have to "beg their living from door to door," he drowned them both in the cellar of his house, which was constantly full of water from a spring. He was convicted and sentenced to be hanged at the Croydon Assizes. During his last few days he was scarcely ever seen without a Bible in his hand, and so sanctimonious and resigned was his bearing that prayers were offered for him in churches in London, and in many parts of the country. On the scaffold he met his death with "great penitency and remorse of conscience."

Richard Corbet, created Dean of Christchurch by Charles I, was born at Ewell in 1582. He was chiefly famous for his wit and learning, and his eloquence as a preacher attracted the notice of James I, who appointed him to be one of his chaplains. From Christchurch he was raised to Oxford, and in 1632 translated to Norwich, in the Choir of whose Cathedral he was buried in 1635.

Besides the flour mills already referred to, there is another industry close to the grounds of Ewell Castle. Here a valuable earth is dug from a huge pit and baked into fire-bricks, and here the tile-bricks referred to elsewhere were manufactured in former days. Other pits in the village have produced quite a quantity of **The Roman** Roman Pottery. Pieces of Samian, and **Discoveries.** complete vases of grey ware have been discovered, and are now in the British Museum. These small vases were probably belonging to a hypocaust, being placed round the large jar containing the bones of some Roman citizen or soldier. The quantity of bones and pottery discovered here points to its having been a burial ground, possibly near a Roman village.

Ewell Castle, a castellated house in the Early Vic**Traces of** torian Gothic style, with stuccoed walls **Nonsuch** and octagonal turrets, is the residence of **Palace.** Mr. A. W. Gadesden. The grounds adjoin Nonsuch Park, and contain the raised foundations of the Banqueting Hall of Nonsuch Palace, with the position of the corner towers plainly shown. Some cellars were also dug out, but have been filled in as before. The park can be entered by a footpath not far from the Brighton Station, or by going along the London Road towards Morden to the lodge gate. The last leads into a splendid avenue traversing the whole park, and emerging on to a road close to Cheam village, passing the modern house built in much the same style as Ewell Castle, the seat of Capt. W. R. G. Farmer, J.P.

Not far from the house there may still be seen a ditch known as Diana's Dyke. The stump of a large elm, probably as old as the days of Elizabeth, can be remembered by those still living as a fine flourishing tree. It was reduced to its present condition during a gale, and the portion of the trunk left standing was further shattered by some mischievous person having blown it up with gunpowder.

[P. 155 - 4 pages back]

P. 151 "3 pages over"

Nonsuch stands in the parish of Cuddington, but no village of Cuddington exists to-day, and it is in connection with the disappearance of the hamlet that one finds the early history of Nonsuch Palace. Henry VIII was for some reason struck with the appearance of the undulating wooded land between Hampton Court and Cheam, and he determined to convert this extensive strip of

The building of Nonsuch Palace.

THE FOUNDATIONS OF THE BANQUETING HALL OF NONSUCH PALACE, IN THE GROUNDS OF EWELL CASTLE.

The plan in the corner shows the form of the building, with its corner towers.

country into a huge park, and erect in it a sumptuous palace. Cuddington Church and Manor House, and whatever other buildings belonged to the hamlet were in the way, and Henry VIII seems to have purchased the estate and destroyed all the buildings upon it, for there are no traces of Church or Manor House to-day. The park appears to have been divided into three portions, two of them named after the palace, and the other called

Worcester Park, after Worcester House.   The purchase took place in 1538, and the King commenced
building his new palace at once, for a considerable
portion was constructed at his death in 1547.   Mary
seems to have had insufficient means to finish the
huge undertaking, and would probably have pulled it
down if Henry, Earl of Arundel, had not undertaken
the work of completing the building "for the love and
honour that he bore to his olde master."   He bought
the two parks and finished the palace, giving it the
fancy name Henry VIII had wished it to be called.

The most complete description of the buildings is
given in the Survey taken by the Parliament during the
Commonwealth in 1650.   I have taken several extracts
from a reprint of the Survey published in 1768.

"*A Survey of Nonsuch House and Park, cum perti-
nentiis, Anno Domini 1650.   Read at the Society of
Antiquaries, Nov. 26, 1768.   From the Original in the
Augmentation Office.*

"A survey of the capitall messuage and royall
mansion house, commonly called Nonsuch, and of the
Parke wherein it stands, and of all the houses and lands
thereunto belonging, situate lying & being in the
county of Surry, late percell of the possessions and
joynture lands of Henrietta Maria, the relict and late
wife of Charles Stuart, late king of England, made
& taken by us whose names are hereunto subscribed,
in the month of April, Anno Domini 1650, by virtue of
a commission grounded upon an act of the Commons
assembled in parliament for the sale of the honors,
manors, & lands of the late king, queen, & prince,
under the hands & seals of five or more of the trustees
in the said act named & appointed :

"All that capitall messuage or royall mansion house,
with the appurtenances, commonly called Nonsuch,
scytuate, standing & being in or near the middle parte
of the little Parke of Nonsuch in the said County of
Surry, consisting of one fayer stronge & large
structure or building of free stone of two large stories
high, well wrought & battled with stone & covered

with blue slate, standing round a court of 150 foote long & 132 foote broad, paved with stone, commonly called the Outward Courte. The lower of which stories contains severall necessary & very usefull rooms, formerly used for severall offices, as the buttery, the wine cellar, three rooms belonging to the lady Holland's servants, six rooms for the housekeeper, three rooms for the gentlemen ushers and quarter wayter, two rooms for the groom porter, and one room for Mr. Henry Seremin. The higher storie contains three rooms, formerly the lady Denbigh's, groome of the stoole, two rooms for the maids of honour, three rooms for the lady Holland, a dining room with a drawing roome, and a bed chamber for the lady Carlisle, two rooms for her servants, two rooms for the queen's almner, four rooms for the lord Dorset, lord chamberlain, & two roomes for the house keeper.

" Memorandum, that the gatehouse leading into the outward court aforesaid, is a building very stronge and gracefull being three stories high, leaded over head, battled & turretted in every of the four corners thereof, the highest of which stories contains a very large & spacious roome, very pleasant & delectable for prospect.

" And also consisting of one other faire & very curious structure or building of two stories high, the lowest story whereof is of good & well wrought free stone, and the higher of wood, richly adorned & set forth & garnished with variety of statues, pictures, & other antick formes of excellent art and workmanship, and of no small cost ; all which building lying allmost upon a square, is covered with blue slate, and incloseth one faire large court of one hundred thirty seaven foot broad, and one hundred and sixteen foot long, all paved with free stone, commonly called the Inner Court : the lower of which stories contains one roome called the Guard Chamber, two roomes for the lady Cary, two roomes for madam nurse, one roome called the Queen's Back Stairs, two roomes for Madame Vautlet, the queen's dresser, two roomes for doctor Myerne, two roomes for Madame Conget, two roomes

for the queen's priests, two roomes for the master of
the horse, two roomes for the queen's robes, two roomes
for madam Cyvet, two roomes for the queen's querries,
the queen's privy kitchen, one roome for Mr. Cooke,
and one other roome for the queen's wayters, the
higher storie conteynes certeine roomes called the
Presence Chamber, the Privy Closet, the Privy Chamber,
the Queen's Back Stayers, the King's Bed Chamber,
the King's Back Stayers, the Queen's Chapell, and two
roomes for the lady marquesse Hambleton.

"Memorandum, that all the roomes comprised within
the said last mentioned building are very faire and large,
many of them being wainscotted round & matted,
& adorned with spacious lights both inwards &
outwards, guarded with iron barrs & all of them fitt
for present use.

"Memorandum, Allso that the Inward Court aforesaid,
stands higher than the said Outward Court by an assent
of eight steps leading therefrom through a Gate House
of free stone three stories high, leaded and turretted in
the four corners, in the middle of which Gate house
stands a clock case turretted and leaded all over,
wherein is placed a clock and a bell; this last mentioned
Gate House standing as aforesaid in the middle betwixt
the said Outward & Inward Courts, is of most excellent
workmanship & a very speciall ornament to Nonsuch
house.

"Memorandum, Also that the said Inner Courte is
battled on the outsides thereof with frames of wood all
covered with lead and supported with strong barrs of
iron, also covered with lead & fixed to the master
pannes of the building, which battlements are a very
great grace & special ornament to the whole building.
On the East & West corners of which said Inner Court
building, there are placed two large & well built turrets
of five stories high, each of them containing five
roomes, besides their staircases, the highest of which
roomes, together with the lanthorns above the same,
are covered with lead and battled round with frames of
wood covered with lead ; these turrets command the
prospect & view of both the parkes of Nonsuch, &

of most of the country round about, and are the cheife ornament of the whole house of Nonsuch.

"That in the said Inner Court, and neare about the middle thereof, there is placed one faire fountaine of white marble, supported by two brass dragons, under which is a large square cistern of lead, set within a frame of white marble, unto which cisterne is an assent of three stepps, over against the South side of which fountaine the aforesaid privy gallery doth lie, being a roome waynscotted & matted & very pleasant ; in the middle of which is a belcone of very good workmanship placed over against the said fountaine.

"Memorandum, that in the said privy garden there is one piramide in spired pinacle of marble, set upon a basis of marble grounded upon a rise of free stone, near unto which on the West side of the said West turret, there is placed one large marble wash boule or bason, over which stands a marble pellican, fed with a pipe of lead to convey water into the same. There are also two other marble pinnacles or piramides called the Pawlcon perches, betwixt which is placed a fountaine of white marble with a lead cesterne, which fountaine is set round with six trees called lelack* trees, which trees beare no fruite but only a very pleasant flower. There are in the said privy garden, one hundred & forty fruit trees, two ewe trees, one juniper tree, six lelack trees, in the said kitchen garden and old orchard, seventy two fruit trees & one faire lime tree, all which materials of the said privy garden & premises are comprised within the gross values of the materials of Nonsuch house as apperteyning thereunto.

"And also consisting of one structure of timber building of a quadrengular forme, pleasantly scituated upon the highest parte of the said Nonsuch Parke, commonly called the Banquetting House, being compassed round with a brick wall, the four corners whereof represent four half moons or fortified angles ; this building being of three stories high, conteines three faire cellars, for the first storye one large hall waynscotted, and three other roomes for the second storye, and five roomes for

---

* These were some of the first lilacs planted in England.

the third storye, most of them all waynscotted &
lighted quite round the whole house, the stanchions
out postes of which banquetting house are all covered
with lead ; over the third story there is a lanthorne
placed, covered with lead, & in every of the four
corners of the whole house a belcone placed for
prospect.

"Memorandum, unto this Banquetting house belongs
one little building, containing a bakehouse and a roome
wherein is placed a faire well with a wheele for winding
up of water, & one other little house used for a wash
house ; both which buildings stand in the said Nonsuch
Parke, opposite to the gate leading to the said banquetting house.

"And also consisting of one other pile of timber
building tyled over head, near adjoyning to Nonsuch
House, on the East side thereof usually belonging to
the under house keeper *(de bene placite)* conteyning a
hall, a kitchen, a buttery, a milke house, a parler, a
cellar and six roomes above stairs, one little garden,
& one little orchard.

" And also consisting one little timber building, tyled
over head, near adjoyning to the said under house
keeper's house, commonly called the Saucery House,
conteyning foure little roomes used by the yeomen of
the Sauces.

"And also consisting of one brick building near
adjoyning to the said saucery house, commonly called
the Well House, within which house is a faire well of a
great depth, a large cesterne of lead, and a wheele for
winding up the water with two large & strong buckets
well bound with iron.

"The said capitall messuage or mansion house, and
all the said other houses & buildings belonging to the
same, scituate & being with the said Nonsuch Parke,
are generally in very good repayer, & not fit to be
demolished or taken down, yet in regard we have made
no yearly value of the same, wee have proceeded to a
full & perfect view of all the materialls thereof, both
within & without the same as they stand respectively ;
& having particularly apprised the same, we do find

that the materialls of all houses & premises before the
mentioned are worth, to be sold, above all charges to
be allowed for taking down the same, in stone, tymber,
lead, slate, tyle, bricks, iron, glass, wainscott, cesternes,
fountaines, fruit trees, & other the before mentioned
utensils & premisses upon the place, the sum of
7020£."

From other writers at different periods there are less
detailed descriptions of the Palace. Leland, who wrote
in the reign of Henry VIII, says in the notes to his

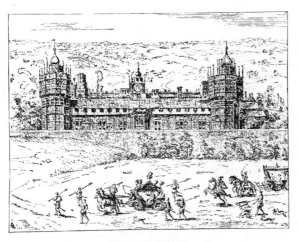

NONSUCH PALACE.
From the Engraving by Houfnagle.

Cygnea Cantio, "Here Henry VIII, in his magnificence,
erected a structure so beautiful, so elegant, and so
splendid, that in whatever direction the admirer of
florid architecture turns his eyes, he will say that it
easily bears off the prize. So great is the emulation
of ancient Roman art, such are its paintings, its gilding,
and its decoration of all kinds, that you would say that
it is the sky spangled with stars. Long life to a king

L

who spares no expense that the ingenuity of his artists may exhibit such wonders, which ravish the minds, and the gaze of mankind by their magnificence."

Camden, in his "Britannia," wrote in much the same strain. Paul Hentzner, who was in England in 1598 as tutor to a German nobleman, wrote a description of Nonsuch in Latin, and an English version of this was published in 1757. "In the pleasure and artificial gardens," he writes, "are many columns and pyramids of marble, with two fountains that spout water one round the other like a pyramid. Upon it are perched small birds, that stream water out of their bills. In the grove of Diana is an agreeable fountain, with Actæon turned into a stag, as he was sprinkled by the goddess and her nymphs, with inscriptions. There is, besides, another pyramid of marble, full of concealed pipes, which spurt upon all who come within their reach."

Water gardens somewhat of this type may still be seen as near to Nonsuch as Wotton, the seat of the Evelyns between Dorking and Leith Hill. In Braun's "Cities of the World," published at Cologne in 1682, there is a view of "Nonciutz—c'est à dire, Non-pareil," by Houfnagle, and according to this work it was one of the wonders of the world, Henry VIII having "procured many excellent artificers, architects, sculptors and statuaries, as well Italian, French and Dutch as natives, who all applied to the ornament of this mansion the finest and most curious skill they possessed in their several arts, embellishing it both within and without, with magnificent statues, some of which vividly represent the antiquities of Rome and some even surpass them."

When Nonsuch belonged to Henrietta Maria, mother of Charles II, Evelyn visited the Palace. On Jan. 3rd, 1666, he writes :—

"I supped in None-Such House, whither the office of the Exchequer was transferred during the plague, at my good friend's Mr. Packe's, and took an exact view of the plaster statues and bass relievos inserted 'twixt

Evelyn's
Account of
Nonsuch.

[P. 163 - 4 pages back]

the timbers and punchions of the outside walls of the
Court ; which must needs have been the work of some
celebrated Italian. I much admired how it had lasted
so well and intire since the time of Henry VIII, exposed
as they are to the aire ; and pitty it is they are not
taken out and preserv'd in some drie place ; a gallerie
would become them. There are some mezzo-relievos
as big as the life, the storie is of the Heathen Gods,
emblems, compartments etc. The Palace consists of
two courts, of which the first is of stone, Castle-like,
by the Lo. Lumlies (of which 'twas purchased), the
other of timber, a Gothic fabric, but these walls incom-
parably beautified. I observ'd that the appearing
timber punchions, entrelices, etc. were all so cover'd
with scales of slate, that it seemed carv'd in the wood
and painted, the slate fastened on the timber in pretty
figures, that has, like a coate of armour, preserv'd it
from rotting. There stand in the garden two handsome
stone pyramids, and the avenue planted with rows of
faire elmes, but the best of these goodly trees, both of
this and of Worcester Park adjoyning, were fell'd by
those destructive and avaricious rebells in the late warr,
which defaced one of the stateliest seates his Majesty
had.''

Pepys, writing in 1663, says : " We went through
Nonesuch Parke to the house, and there viewed as much
as we could of the outside, and looked through the
great gates, and found a noble court ; and altogether
believe it to have been a very noble house, and a delicate
parke about it, where just now there was a doe killed
for the King to carry up to Court."

The Earl of Arundel having completed the Palace he
was able to receive Queen Elizabeth on one of her
" Progresses " in 1559. It was in the sultry month of
August, and it must have struck her as being a particularly lovely spot, with its fine trees and healthy breezes
from the Downs, for she paid further visits in 1567,
1569 and 1580, and a few years later purchased of Lord
Lumley the Palace and Little Park, subsequently
spending much of her time there, in hunting and other
amusements.

L 2

A rather remarkable incident took place while the Queen was in residence at Nonsuch. It is given in a letter from Rowland White to Sir Robert Sydney, dated Nonsuch, September, 1599, published in the Sydney State Papers (vol. II) :—

"Vpon Michaelmas Eve, about 10 a clock in the morning, my Lord of Essex 'lighted at Court Gate in Post, and made all hast up to the Presence, and soe to the Privy Chamber, and staied not till he came to the Queens Bed Chamber, where he found the Queen newly up, the Hare about her Face ; he kneeled vnto her, kissed her Hands, and had some private Speach with her, which seemed to give him great Contentment ; for coming from her Majestie to go shifte hymself in his Chamber, he was very pleasant, and thancked God, though he had suffered much Trouble and Storms Abroad, he found a sweet Calm at Home. 'Tis much wondred at here, that he went so boldly to her Majesties Presence, she not being ready, and he soe full of Dirt and Mire, that his very face was full of yt. About 11 he was ready, and went vp againe to the Queen, and conferred with her till half an Howre after 12. As yet all was well, and her Vsage very gracious towards hym." . . . Until this time the Queen had shewn no displeasure, but when (after his dinner), he again went into her presence, he "found her much changed in that small Tyme, for she began to call hym to question for his Return, and was not satisfied in the Manner of his coming away, and leaving all Things at soe great hazard. She apointed the Lords to heare hym, and soe they went to Cownsell in the After noone,—and he went with them where they satt an Howre. But nothing was determined or yet known ; belike yt is referred to a full Cownsell, for all the Lords are sent for, to be here this Day. Yt is mistrustful that for his Disobedience he shall be comytted." On the same night "between 10 and 11 a clock, a Commandment came from the Queen, to my Lord of Essex, that he should keepe his Chamber ; and on the following Monday he was committed to the custody of the Lord Keeper, at York House."

In the following year Essex was in open rebellion against the Queen, and shortly afterwards his career was terminated upon Tower Hill.

After the death of Elizabeth the Palace and Little Park were settled upon Anne, the Queen of James I, who seems to have been anxious to obtain the Great Park as well as the Little, and eventually purchased it from Lord Lumley. Charles I held the whole estate until it was taken over by the Parliament, and after the execution of the unfortunate monarch the Commissioners appointed to dispose of the Crown lands granted a lease of Nonsuch House to Algernon Sydney at a rent of £150 a year. At the Restoration, however, Charles II required possession of the House and Parks from the various persons into whose hands they had fallen. Henrietta Maria became possessed of the Cuddington portion, and on Sept. 5th, 1660, she granted the office

LADY CASTLEMAINE, BARBARA VILLIERS, DUCHESS OF CLEVELAND,

The despoiler of Nonsuch Palace.

From an Engraving of Sir Peter Lely's Picture.

of keeper of the House of Nonsuch and of the Little Park to George Lord Berkeley. After the death of Henrietta Maria the whole estates, including Nonsuch Palace and Worcester House, passed through various hands until Barbara Villiers, Countess of Castlemaine, mistress of Charles II, was created Baroness of Nonsuch and Duchess of Cleveland.   Finding the Palace expen-

The demolition of the Palace. sive, this magnificent pile, which had passed through the Commonwealth unscathed, was pulled down by the Duchess, together with Worcester House—the Park being cut up into farms.   It was just at this time (1670 to 1680) that Epsom was growing so rapidly, and this enormous quantity of building material was at once bought up and utilised in many of the larger houses of the town, the greater portion of it being incorporated into the Earl of Berkeley's new house—Durdans. Unfortunately this building does not exist to-day, Lord Rosebery's seat being of much later date.

Pit Place, close to Epsom Parish Church, contains a quantity of carved stone and marble, and there is much for and little against the belief that it was brought there from Nonsuch.   St. Martin's Rectory, "Silver Birches," the residence of Dr. Daniel, and "Rosebank" in South Street, all have traces of Nonsuch in the richly moulded woodwork of their interiors, but these houses are all treated in greater detail in Chapter V.

Some barns at Ewell are remembered to have contained some carved beams in their roofs, but they were pulled down many years ago.

At the eastern lodge gates of Nonsuch Park there

Cheam Village. stands a stone cross over a drinking fountain erected in 1895 by "G. and M. Farmer" and this is quite close to Cheam village.   Until recently this could claim to be an wholly unspoiled and thoroughly rural little hamlet, but it is now painfully apparent that this is no longer the case.   One of the most attractive spots in the village was at the main cross-roads, where a pretty collection of cottages, some of them behind little rustic gardens, high red brick walls, and a white direction post, made a charming picture.   Now in place of much of this picturesqueness a tall, square block of shop buildings has been substi-tuted—a more painful piece of vandalism one can scarcely imagine, and the new cast-iron direction post merely heightens the impression.   Fortunately Cheam is not entirely spoilt.   Towards the Church there is

plenty of unviolated antiquity. One first passes on the left a low, half-timbered gable end overhanging the pavement in quite an unexpected manner; further on there is Cheam House, a large red brick building with a classic front, and opposite the high brick walls on the right is a timber house of great age. It is variously called "White Hall" and "Maids of Honour House," and is the subject of more than one tradition, but there seems little doubt that it dates from the days of Henry VIII. The rooms are full of heavy oaken beams, the outer walls are boarded and painted white, and the windows are filled with leaded glass. The walls of the present drawing-room of the house were until recent years covered with fine tapestry, showing various Elizabethan outdoor sports, and also an elopement in one of the earliest forms of post-chaise. The room, now used as a drawing-room, is believed to have been used as a council chamber by Queen Elizabeth during her long visits to Nonsuch Palace. The adjoining wooden cottage, formerly connected with "White Hall," has a cellar approached by a flight of steps cut in the sandy soil. The least reliable story connected with it states that the cellar led to an underground passage to Nonsuch Palace. Another tradition makes it a secret meeting place for reading the Bible by persecuted Protestants in the days of Mary, and when the tables were turned as a resort of Roman Catholics who said mass equally secretly during the enforcement of the penal laws against Catholics. Close by, on the same side of the road, is the rectory, a fine old red brick house standing in a very pleasant garden backed by large trees. It formerly had a carved inscription on the outside of the dining-room chimney, referring to a rector who was Chaplain to Queen Elizabeth and Bishop of Chichester, but this has become obliterated during the last twenty years. Some of the walls are covered with tile-bricks, probably from the old Ewell pottery, and everything points to its being quite three hundred years old.

Cheam Church, dedicated to St. Dunstan, is a modern building in Early English style, having been rebuilt in

WHITE HALL, CHEAM,
A Sixteenth Century Timber House.

1864. It has a nave, north and south aisles, an apsidal chancel, and a tower and spire at the north-west corner added in 1870. The organ is in a recess at the north of the chancel,

Cheam Church.

with choir vestry on the opposite side separated by an oaken screen. The general impression given by the interior is unusual, the walls being faced with red and black brick relieved with bands of white stone, while the exterior is entirely of stone. The plain circular pillars are of Purbeck marble, with very ornate capitals of rather crude workmanship, while most of the stained glass may be described by the same adjective. The modern font consists of a huge block of stone resting upon stumpy pillars, the alternate ones of green marble.

Out in the churchyard one may see the chancel of the former church, in reality the Lumley Chapel of the building which preceded the one taken down in 1864. From a note, supposed to be in Laud's handwriting, on a pane of glass taken out of Croydon Palace, and now preserved in Lambeth Palace, it is known that " Eccle de Micham, Cheme, et Stone cum aliis fulgure combustiæ sunt Jan. 14, 1638-9," and it is easy to see the results of this or a subsequent fire upon the monument to Jane, Lady Lumley. The large slabs of marble have been fractured by the heat, and one side is very much discoloured. It seems that the Lumley Chapel and portions of the chancel walls and tower were saved, and a new church, consisting of nave, aisles, and chancel was built, utilising the Lumley Chapel as a chancel. The Lumley Chapel is always kept locked up, the key being only obtainable at the Rectory.

Against the north wall stands the monument to John, Lord Lumley, It is of white marble, with Corinthian columns on either side, a visored helmet resting on the lower portion. On nineteen shields are the arms of the Lumley family, with their various connections—the popinjay of the Lumleys being very noticeable. The inscription, of great length, in Latin, gives the descent of the Lumleys from Lyulph of Saxon times to the death of Lord Lumley in 1609. He is notable as one of the judges in the trial of Mary, Queen of Scots, and

as the originator of the curious collection of monuments
of his ancestors in the church of Chester-le-Street, near
Lumley Castle, Durham,

In a recess in the same wall as Lord Lumley's monument is that to his second wife, Elizabeth, daughter of

THE BRASS REPRESENTING THE TRINITY, FROM THE TOMB OF
THOMAS FROMOND, IN THE LUMLEY CHAPEL AT CHEAM,
AND A PORTION OF A PALIMPSEST, SHOWING ST. JOHN WITH THE
POISONED CHALICE.

John, Lord D'Arcy of Chiche. The figure is finely
carved in alabaster. His first wife, Jane, daughter of
Henry Fitzalan, Earl of Arundel, lies beneath the altar
tomb already mentioned. She was a distinguished
Greek scholar, having translated into English the

"Iphigenia" of Euripides and some of the orations of Isocrates. There are many other monuments of interest, but the brasses are especially noticeable ; among them are preserved those taken from the Fromond Chapel when it was pulled down. On being removed from its decayed stone slab, the almost barbaric representation of the Trinity shown in the accompanying drawing was found to be a palimpsest, the under side showing that it was cut out of another brass of a much larger size. It was inserted in the monument to Thomas Fromond, who died in 1542. The inscription runs :—

> "Pray for the Soulles of Thomas Fromond Esquyer and Elizabeth his wyffe, daughter and heyer of John Yerde Esquyer whiche Thomas decessyd the XXIst day of March, the yer of or Lord God MVcXLII, and in the XXXIIId yere of the reygne of Kynge Henry the VIIIth, On whose Soulles J'hu have mercy, a . . ."

The under side of another small brass shows St. John with the poisoned chalice. A nameless brass at the south-east corner is unique in being the smallest representation of a complete figure in brass in this country. The curiously shaped font of the old church, probably dating from some year subsequent to the fire, is still preserved in the Lumley Chapel. It consists of a tall stand resembling that of a sun-dial supporting a thin stone basin about two feet in diameter. A large brass on the east wall is to the memory of "Edmund Barret, Esq. Serjeant of the wine-cellar to King Charles," who died in 1631, and his eldest son.

The ceiling of the chapel is richly ornamented with popinjays and quatrefoils in plaster, and bears the date 1592.

In the southern part of the churchyard, to the west of the Lumley Chapel, is an altar tomb covered with a slab of black marble, covering the remains of Henry Neale, his wife Christiana, and their daughter, Eliza Dutton, who "was murdered on the 13th of July, 1687, by her neighbour, while endeavouring to make peace between him and his wife." The following lines may be deciphered beneath the inscription :—

> " Here lyes the best of wives, of mothers and of friends
> Whose soul, too good for earth, in heaven attends
> With joy and comfort till the day of doome,
> When all her virtuous deeds shall thither come :
> To save her neighbour she has spilt her blood,
> And like her Saviour died for doing good.
> May that curs'd hand forget itself to feed
> That made its benefactour thus to bleed."

Within the high red brick walls on the south of the churchyard there formerly stood the manor house of the Earls of Bedford. It was unfortunately pulled down more than a century ago and a paper factory was built upon its site. The industry seems to have failed many years ago, but the villagers still speak of " the factory walls," forgetting their original use. One relic of the manor house remains in the circular red brick dove cote, with its delightful wooden lantern.

What is probably the oldest private school in England still exists at Cheam. It seems to have suddenly grown important during the prevalence of the Great Plague in 1665, when, according to Brayley, several people sent their children to Cheam, to a gentleman who kept a small school in " Whitehall House." This building was most probably situated nearly opposite to Cheam House, where a fine old wrought-iron gate now stands. The school seems to have existed for some time before this near London, and was removed to Cheam during the Plague, continuing without interruption until about 1719, when the Rev. Dr. Sanxay built the present school standing in the main street of the village. He was succeeded by his son, who became Rector of Sutton, resigning the school to the Rev. William Gilpin, the celebrated writer on the picturesque, whose "Forest Scenery" was published in 1791, and who has been immortalised as " Dr. Syntax." After passing under the rule of the Rev. William Giffin, junr., and the Rev. James Wilding, the school was taken in 1827 by Dr. Mayo, who taught on the Pestalozzian system, having studied Pestalozzi's principles during his residence at the establishment at Yverdun as English chaplain. The present head master is Mr. A. S. Tabor,

Cheam School.

Quite a number of distinguished scholars have been educated at Cheam School.   Henry Addington, afterwards Viscount Sidmouth ; Dr. Waldegrave, Bishop of Carlisle ; the Right Honourable Hugh Childers ; Lord Hobart, Governor of Madras ; Sir James Fergusson, Governor of South Australia, Marquis of Bath ; the Earl of Donoughmore, Lord Dundonald, the Earl of Carrick, Lord Aberdeen and Lord Russell all received their early education here.   Some idea of the notoriety of Cheam School may be obtained from a conversation Madame D'Arblay records in her diary between George III, Queen Charlotte and herself :

> "Where will she send him?" said the King.   The Queen, looking at me with a smile, answered, "To the school where Mr. Locke puts his sons ; I know that!"   "And where is that?"   "Indeed, I don't know; where is it, Miss Burney?" "At Cheam, ma'am."   "Oh, at young Gilpin's?" cried the King.   "Is it near Mr. Locke's?"   "Yes, sir ; within about six miles, I believe."

From Cheam to Mr. Locke's seat, Norbury Park, was more than six miles, but Miss Burney's hurried calculation may be excused on account of some natural nervousness in addressing the King.   The house was raised a storey some years ago, and in 1867 a detached chapel was built.

Besides the village of Cheam there are other districts known as North Cheam, Cheam Common, Lower Cheam and Belmont, Lower Cheam House having been formerly held by the Fromond family before mentioned.   In the Domesday Survey Cheam is given as *Ceiham*, and a church is mentioned as existing then.   The descent of the various manors of Cheam may be found in Brayley's as well as in Manning and Bray's histories of Surrey.

The remote hamlet of Chessington (in other days known as Chessingdon) may be reached *Chessington* from Ewell by following the road past the South-Western Station, meeting, after a little over a mile, the junction with the Hook Road from Epsom. Three-quarters of a mile from this point a little tributary of the Hogsmill River runs across the roadway, the footpath being carried by a light wooden bridge. By the side of this bridge and some pollard willows

stands a little inn, picturesquely placed, and curiously
named "Bone's Gate," having a five-barred gate as a
sign, the inscription upon it reading

> This gate hangs well
> And hinders none,
> Refresh and pay
> And travel on.

Just beyond this attractive little spot a turning to the
left by a pond leads up to Chessington. The village
consists of the Church, a farm, some cottages, and the
large house known as Chessington Hall. Although
restored considerably, the little church with its diminu-
tive spire perched on the roof ridge is interesting, its
delightful situation giving it a special charm. Standing
in the porch one has a view through an opening in the
trees which line the roadway across the green meadows
in the foreground, to Epsom lying snugly beneath the
shelter of the Downs. Eastward the view extends
beyond Banstead, and westwards the country seems
covered with forests to the horizon at Headley and
Ranmore. The Horton Asylum is unfortunately prominent in the middle distance.

The Church, dedicated to St. Mary, contains a
nave, a chancel, and a south aisle separated
from the nave by double wooden pillars.
The original building was Norman, but the
restoration of 1854 has given the structure an Early
English character which is somewhat misleading on a
superficial glance. The original Norman building con-
sisted of a chancel and a nave about half the length of
the present one, the chancel arch being scarcely more
than four feet wide. There seems to have been also a
small south transept. From the untouched Norman
windows still remaining it is plain that the original little
building was of very rude workmanship. Some of these
are not arched with stone in the usual fashion, but are
merely rectangular openings, the upper portion being
supported with a lintel of oak. An ancient aumry,
having a groove for a shelf and hinge brackets, and a
restored fragment of an elaborately carved and painted
stone reredos dug up in the graveyard, are in the

chancel. Another unrestored fragment of the reredos is preserved in the vestry opening out of the north side of the chancel. The modern pews, of oak, follow exactly the pattern of a very old pew-end discovered during the restoration, and now inserted near the door-way in the south aisle. Brayley speaks of a piece of oak lattice discovered in one of the chancel pews, probably belonging to a confessional, and this is still preserved in the vestry. The mouldings round the lattice and panels have recently been pronounced to belong to a period subsequent to the Reformation, so that Brayley's statement must be accepted with reserve. A painted board in the vestry, dated 1628, records the liberal charities of Henry Smith, an Alderman of London, who devoted the income of his estates at Worth and Balcombe in Sussex to the benefit of the worthy poor. On the north wall of the nave are two very similar plain marble monuments, one of them to the memory of Samuel Crisp, the devoted friend of Dr. Burney and Fanny—Madame D'Arblay. The eulogistic inscription was written by Dr. Burney on the death of his old friend on April 24th, 1783.

> Reader this cold and humble spot contains
> The much lamented, much rever'd Remains
> Of one whose Wisdom, Learning, Taste, and Sense,
> Good-humour'd Wit and wide Benevolence
> Chear'd and enlighten'd all this Hamlet round,
> Where ever Genius, Worth, or Want was found.
> To few it is that bounteous Heav'n imparts
> Such depth of Knowledge and such Taste in Arts ;
> Such Penetration, and Enchanting Pow'rs
> Of bright'ning social and Convivial Hours.
> Had he, through Life, been blest by Nature kind
> With Health robust of Body, as of Mind,
> With skill to serve and charm Mankind so great
> In arts, in Science, Letters, Church, or State,
> His Name the Nation's annals had enrolled
> And virtues to remotest ages told.
>   C. BURNEY.

It is impossible to turn to the adjoining monument to Mrs. Frances Dalrymple, so similar in appearance but of a later date, without a smile, for beneath the name is the brief information that

> "The Exalted mind requires no panegyrick to its fame."

Near the porch and facing the font is a tablet to the memory of Mrs. Sarah Hamilton. The font is much restored, but the circular base and one of the marble supports are old.

Quite close to the Church, on the same ridge, stands Chessington Hall, rebuilt on the foundations of the house, to which Samuel Crisp retreated after the failure of his tragedy "Virginia," although the reason for his retirement has been attributed to a straitened income and gout. Chessington is remote now, but about

Samuel Crisp and the Burneys.

FANNY BURNEY (MADAM D'ARBLAY).
From the Painting made at Chessington Hall by her cousin, Edward Burney.

1760 Macaulay says that no road or sheep walk connected it with the abodes of men. To his old friends the Burneys he alone entrusted the secret of his retreat. He looked upon Fanny as his daughter, affectionately calling her his "Fannikin," while she in return called him her "dear Daddy." In her diary there are constant references to visits to Chessington, described as "this ever dear place." On Monday, August 12th, 1782,

Fanny Burney.

she writes of a visit to Chessington with her cousin Edward, who was to make some portraits of Mr. Crisp. "The instant dinner was over," she writes, "to my utter surprise and consternation, I was called into the room appropriated for Edward and his pictures, and informed I was to sit to him for Mr. Crisp!" The portrait reproduced here is from an engraving of the picture made on this occasion.

Fanny Burney was at Chessington during Mr. Crisp's last illness, and only returned to her father's house in St. Martin Street, Leicester Square, after the burial of her "Daddy" in the churchyard at Chessington. During her five long years of slavery as Lady of the Wardrobe to Queen Charlotte, a subject on which Macaulay could scarcely write with moderation, so intense was his disgust at the virtual burying alive of the talented authoress of "Evelina," Fanny Burney visited Chessington Hall for a few hours. On returning to town she writes, "I left them all with great reluctance. I had no time to walk in the garden, no heart to ascend the little mount, and see how Norbury Hills and Woods looked from it." It was on a visit to Norbury Park that Miss Burney met General D'Arblay, who was stopping at Juniper Hall, near Mickleham, with a number of the French refugees who swarmed in England at this time, forced to leave their country during the Revolution. As Madame D'Arblay she produced her third novel, "Camilla," and it may be more than a coincidence that an adjoining estate to Norbury was then, as it is now, known as Camilla Lacey. In the grounds of Chessington Hall stands a quaint little thatched summer house, which was there in Miss Burney's time, and is locally believed to have been one of her favourite haunts, and indeed the quotation already given in which she writes of being unable to ascend the little mount seems to refer to this summer house. It is higher than the rest of the garden, and is

M

approached by some brick steps, while the view undoubtedly includes Norbury Park and the neighbouring
woods and hills.

Buried in a small wood and only reached by footpaths, there is a Roman Camp of considerable size and in good preservation. The
easiest way to reach it from the Church is
by going down the lane towards the Kings-
ton Road for a short distance until a footpath marked to
the Ewell Road appears on the right. This leads over
a brook to near the wood enveloping the earth works.
The discoveries made there have been unimportant, the
only authentic one being a single Roman coin.

A succession of meandering footpaths will lead one
all the way to Epsom from Chessington, and although
still unobtrusively pretty, they have been seriously
interfered with by the London County Council's
mammoth lunatic asylum adjoining the tiny hamlet of
Horton. The gaunt yellow brick walls and blue slate
roofs seen through the trees are a cheerless sight, and
one longs for the lusty creepers so seldom allowed to
temper the external austerity of such institutions.

The half-dozen cottages composing Horton stand in
a bowery little by-lane leading out into the Kingston
and Leatherhead road. Crossing this lane at right
angles, the footpaths at length emerge into the open
meadows by the South-Western Station at Epsom.
Another series of footpaths—far prettier than those
just mentioned—lead from Chessington Church south-
westward, passing a sequestered farmstead, and the
derelict Manor House of Horton, the former seat of the
Trotters. Traversing a wood one enters a quiet road
known as Love Lane, which leads out on to Epsom
Common, not far from Christ Church.

CHAPTER XI.

ON THE BIRDS OF EPSOM AND
THE DISTRICT.

THE following list contains the names of all the species of birds known to have occurred within the radius dealt with in this work. The letters in brackets indicate the character of each species' distribution. R. = resident; W.V. = winter visitor; S.M. = summer migrant; O.V. = occasional visitor or straggler. A few notes have been appended to some of the rarer species giving some information as to the locality where they have been noticed.

Missel Thrush (R.)
Song Thrush (R.)
Redwing (W.V.)
Fieldfare (W.V.)
Blackbird (R.)
Ring Ouzel (O.V.) Sometimes seen on the high ground near Banstead and Headley—distinctly rare.
Wheatear (S.M.)
Whinchat (S.M.)
Stonechat (R.) A good many leave in autumn and return in spring.
Redstart (S.M.)
Robin (R.)
Nightingale (S.M.)
Hedge-sparrow (R.)
Whitethroat (S.M.)
Lesser Whitethroat (S.M.)
Garden Warbler (S.M.)
Blackcap (S.M.)
Dartford Warbler (O.V.) Used to nest and may perhaps still do so on the furze-commons. Sometimes seen still, but is very rare. Properly speaking a resident.

Sedge Warbler (S.M.)

Grasshopper Warbler (S.M.) Still often heard and seen on the commons.

Chiffchaff (S.M.)

Willow Warbler (S.M.)

Wood Warbler (S.M.)

Golden-crested Wren (R.)

Long-tailed Tit (R.)

Great Tit (R.)

Blue Tit (R.)

Coal Tit (R.)

Marsh Tit (R.)

Nuthatch (R.)

Tree-creeper (R.)

Wren (R.)

Golden Oriole (O.V.) Very rare; in summer only; has been noticed at Leatherhead.

Starling (R.)

Jay (R.)

Magpie (R.) It is very rarely that a nest is found so close to London: even as a visitor it is getting extremely scarce.

Jackdaw (R.)

Carrion Crow (R.) Nests are rarely found and the bird is mainly a winter visitor.

Hooded Crow (W.V.) Seldom noticed.

Rook (R.)

Great Grey Shrike (O.V.) A very rare visitor to the high grounds in winter.

Red-backed Shrike (S.M.)

Waxwing (O.V.) Has been shot once at Epsom.

Spotted Flycatcher (S.M.)

Swallow (S.M.)

Martin (S.M.)

Sand Martin (S.M.)

Greenfinch (R.)

Hawfinch (R.) Not very uncommon in the wooded district.

Goldfinch (R.) A rare nesting species, but more often seen in winter.

Siskin (W.V.) Rather rare.

House-sparrow (R.)

Tree-sparrow (R.) Chiefly known as a winter visitor of somewhat irregular appearance. Used to and may still nest in a few places in the district.

Chaffinch (R.)

Brambling (W.V.) Of very irregular appearance.

Linnet (R.)

Lesser Redpoll (W.V.) Has sometimes also nested in the district, but not often.

Twite (W.V.) Very rarely observed.

Bullfinch (R.)

Crossbill (W.V.) Not very often noticed.

Corn Bunting (R.)

Yellow Hammer (R.)

Cirl Bunting (R.) A scarce and very local species.

Reed Bunting (R.)

Snow Bunting (O.V.) Very rare : has been seen at Epsom.

Pied Wagtail (R.)

Grey Wagtail (W.V.) Not common.

Yellow Wagtail (S.M.) Comparatively few nest in the district, the bird being seen usually only on its migrations in spring and autumn.

Tree Pipit (S.M.)

Meadow Pipit (R.)

Sky-Lark (R.)

Wood-Lark (R.) Apparently a very rare and local species, doubtless, however, often overlooked.

Swift (S.M.)

Nightjar (S.M.)

Great Spotted Woodpecker (R.) Frequents the old park timbers : not common.

Lesser Spotted Woodpecker (R.) The same remarks apply as in the case of the preceding species.

Green Woodpecker (R.)

Wryneck (S.M.)

Kingfisher (R.) Very few suitable nesting sites in this district, but it has lived at Epsom.

Hoopoe (O.V.) Has been shot and seen at Epsom, and nested once many years ago near Leatherhead.

Cuckoo (S.M.)

Barn Owl (R.)

Long-eared Owl (O.V.) Has been seen and shot and may have nested occasionally in the district : possibly better described as a very rare resident.

Tawny Owl (R.)

Short-eared Owl (O.V.) Has been shot at Headley.

Marsh Harrier (O.V.) Has been shot at Cheam and Headley.

Hen Harrier (O.V.) Has been shot at Headley.

Common Buzzard (O.V.) Two or three have been killed in this district.

Sparrow Hawk (R.) Rare.

Kestrel (R.)

Peregrine Falcon (O.V.) Once captured near Epsom.

Hobby (O.V.) Shot and seen in the district on a few occasions.

Merlin (O.V.) One or two have been taken in the neighbourhood.

Heron (O.V.) Often seen, but there is no heronry in this part of the county : the nearest is at Richmond Park.

Bittern (O.V.) Has been shot three or four times in the neighbourhood.

Mute Swan (R.) A semi-domesticated species.

Sheldrake (O.V.) Once shot at Ashtead : probably an escape from confinement.

Wild Duck (R.) Most of the duck in this neighbourhood are only semi-feral.

Teal (O.V.) Very rarely occurs : no suitable water in the district.

Wigeon (O.V.) Said to have been once shot on Epsom Common : probably an " escape."

Ring-Dove (R.)

Stock-Dove (R.) A great many leave in the autumn.

Turtle-Dove (S.M.)

Pheasant (R.)

Partridge (R.)

Red-legged Partridge (R.)

Quail (O.V.) Very capricious in its appearance, but has occasionally been noticed and may have nested in this district.

Corncrake (S.M.)

Spotted Crake (O.V.) Shot once at Headley.

Water-rail (R.) Not really a resident within the strict area dealt with here, but has sometimes been observed in winter. Breeds on the Mole.

Moorhen (R.)

Coot (R.) Breeds on Leatherhead mill-pond and has sometimes been found in other places in the district.

Stone-Curlew (O.V.) Has been shot on the Downs.

Golden Plover (W.V.)

Asiatic Golden Plover (O.V.) Once shot on Epsom racecourse.

Ringed Plover (O.V.) Has been shot at Headley.

Peewit (R.)

Woodcock (W.V.)

Snipe (W.V.) A few stay and nest sometimes in suitable places such as Epsom Common.

Jack Snipe (W.V.) Rare.

Green Sandpiper (O.V.) A very rare visitor in spring and autumn.

Common Sandpiper (O.V.) Not so rare as the last.

Redshank (O.V.) Has been once shot on Epsom Common.

Black-tailed Godwit (O.V.) Once shot on Epsom Common.

Curlew (O.V.) Often heard on the spring and autumn migrations, and has been seen on the downs.

Whimbrel (O.V.) The same remarks apply.

Common Tern (O.V.) A straggler to the few waters of the district.

Little Tern (O.V.) Rarer than the last, but sometimes shot in the neighbourhood.

Black-headed Gull (O.V.) Another straggler rarely seen so far inland.

Common Gull (O.V.) Small parties sometimes seen in rough weather.

Herring Gull (O.V.)   The same remark applies.
Lesser black-backed Gull (O.V.)   Rarer than the preceding.
Kittiwake (O.V.)   Has been seen occasionally.
Richardson's Skua (O.V.)   Once picked up on Headley heath.
Little Grebe (R.)
Storm Petrel (O.V.)   Once picked up dead at Nork.

A few more species might perhaps be added, and by extending the area to the river Mole and Gatton Park, quite a large number of species would be included.

It might perhaps be worth adding that the Whitethroat is here the Nettle-creeper, the Long-tailed Tit the Bottle-tit, the Red-backed Shrike the Butcher Bird, the Yellow Hammer the Writing-Lark, the Meadow Pipit the Tit-Lark, the Nightjar the Goatsucker or Evejar, the Green Woodpecker the Yaffle, the Wryneck the Cuckoo's mate, the Ring-Dove and Stock-Dove Wood-pigeons or simply Pigeons, the Turtle-Dove simply Dove, and the Peewit the Lapwing or Plover.

JOHN A. BUCKNILL.

CHAPTER XII.

GOLF AT EPSOM.

THOUGH the Epsom Golf Club dates no further back than January, 1889, it may be interesting to place on record, before they are lost in oblivion, a few facts concerning its early days.

It is melancholy (for a golfer) to reflect upon the long period during which the possibilities afforded by the beautiful Epsom Downs remained neglected. Towards the end of the "Eighties" however, came the "great awakening," in which Epsom was not slow to join. To whom belongs the honour of first wielding a club on Epsom Downs? That point will never be decided. Among the first outposts of the army of occupation must be mentioned Dr. Laidlaw Purvis (of the Royal Wimbledon Golf Club), and Mr. Richardson, of Sutton, who for some years before the formation of the Club had "knocked a ball" upon Epsom Downs. To Mr. T. W. Lang, brother of Andrew Lang, belongs the honour of first playing the game in any regular manner. Living at "The Uplands," and often accompanied by Mr. Walter Bovill and other Wimbledonians, he began to play with some regularity about the year '86, playing on rough and ready greens between the Grand Stand and the Rifle Butts.

Somewhat later another Scotsman, a well-known resident of Epsom, Mr. P. Robertson Rodger, would also occasionally practise his national game; and a little later again appeared on the scene Mr. Felix Barry, Mr. F. H. A. Booth, Mr. Gordon Ruck, and other visitors.

Towards the close of '88 the Masters of the College, incited thereto by Mr. Mackey, a colleague from Malvern, mapped out a course near the Downs Station. Residents in Epsom began to try their hands by twos and threes, and a small subscription was collected by one of the Masters of the College to pay for rolling and sweeping the greens.

The time was now ripe for the formation of a Club, and at a preliminary meeting held at Bromley Hurst (then occupied by Mr. G. F. Burgess) on 25th January, 1889, it was resolved that a Club should be formed.

The Club was soon in working order, with an annual subscription of 10/6.

The Lord of the Manor, Mr. J. S. Strange, readily granted the necessary leave to play, and accepted the position of president. No opposition was encountered from the Commoners, of whom several were elected vice-presidents.

It may at once be stated that throughout its history the Club has been treated with the greatest consideration by all those who have rights and interests in the Downs.

Mr. Alexander Patrick, of Wimbledon, was employed to survey and lay out a course, which when adopted included (roughly speaking) the College Masters' course and Mr. Lang's course.

The Club Room (next door to the present "Hussar") soon became inadequate, and it was resolved to rent the picturesque "Beech Cottage" from Mr. John Nightingall in the spring of 1890.

A resident professional was engaged in Arthur Jackson, soon to be succeeded by W. Dunn, and in October, 1890, by Thomas McWatt.

In 1892 the death of Mr. John Nightingall necessitated a move to another Club House. After a brief occupation of "The Bungalow," opposite Beech Cottage, the present excellent house, designed by Mr. J. Hatchard Smith, was erected and completed by October, 1893.

In April, 1893, it was decided to increase the number of members to 200, and to extend the course to Tatten-ham Corner and along the Race-course, abandoning the holes behind the Butts.

The Club has now 250 members, with a large waiting list of candidates. Residents within three miles of the Club House have the preference in election to the extent that two residents are elected for one non-resident. The annual subscription is £2 2s., with an entrance fee of £5 5s.

The present officers are:—President, Hon. Mr. Justice Bucknill; Vice-Presidents, The Earl of Rosebery, Sir Allan Sarle, Mr. Herbert Brooks, Capt. W. R. G. Farmer, Rev. E. W. Northey, Mr. P. Ralli, Mr. J. S. Strange, Mr. R. Walters; Captain, Mr. E. P. Burd; Hon. Treasurer, Mr. A. E. Harter; Hon. Secretary, Jos. F. Smith; Committee, Messrs. W. R. Burgess, A. W. Daniel, S. F. Jackson, R. A. Johnstone, C. P. C. Jones, F. McNair, D. H. Tomkins, H. F. Turner, C. Webb.

The Rosebery Medal (handicap) and the Brooks Cup (scratch) are played for twice a year.

The course is one of the best inland courses, with plenty of variety, sporting greens, charming views, and the very best of air.

EPSOM AND DISTRICT RIFLE CLUB.

This Club was formed, as stated in its rules, "with the object of encouraging Rifle-shooting and Volunteering in the district, and forming a reserve of retired Volunteers and others, unable to make themselves efficient Volunteers, prepared to join with the Volunteers for the purpose of national defence."

The inaugural meeting was held at the Golf Club, on the 26th December, 1899. It will thus be seen that the Club is one of the first, and it is believed the very first, of the new civilian rifle clnbs.

Much assistance was given in the formation of the Club by the Hon. Mr. Justice Bucknill, who was one of the first promoters, and has taken the greatest interest in its welfare.

Candidates for election must reside within the recruiting district of the 2nd Vol. Batt. East Surrey Regiment. Members are allowed to use the Drill Shed of the

Epsom Detachment for Morris Tube shooting, and also the Range on Epsom Downs.

Ordinary members pay a subscription of £1 11s. 6d., which includes a subscription of 10s. 6d. as honorary members of the Epsom Detachment.

The Committee has power to elect extraordinary members with a subscription of 5s., and also boy-members. Ordinary members must have completed their 30th year, and extraordinary members their 35th year before election.

The present officers are : President, the Hon. Mr. Justice Bucknill ; Hon. Treasurer, Capt. Bagshaw, O.C. the Epsom Detachment ; Hon. Secretary, G. F. Burgess ; Committee, Col. Norbury Pott, Lieut.-Col. E. W. Ruck, Major G. F. Ruck, Messrs. B. Braith-waite, E. P. Burd, F. W. Freeman, F. W. Ledger, D. Napper, A. Russell, E. Vassie.

The Club has 100 ordinary and extraordinary members on its roll.

G. F. BURGESS.

CHAPTER XIII.

ROAD DISTANCES FROM EPSOM.

	Miles
Ashtead - - - - - - - -	2
Banstead - - - - - - - -	3½
Betchworth Clump - - - - - -	6½
Bookham, Great - - - - - -	6
,, Little - - - - - -	7
Box Hill, *via* Leatherhead - - - - -	8
,, ,, *via* Headley - - - - -	7½
Burgh Heath - - - - - - -	3
Cheam - - - - - - - -	3
Chessington - - - - - - -	3½
Chipstead - - - - - - -	6½
Croydon - - - - - - -	8½
Dorking - - - - - - -	8½
Effingham - - - - - - -	8
Esher - - - - - - - -	6
Ewell - - - - - - - -	1½
Guildford - - - - - - -	16
Headley - - - - - - -	4½
Horsham - - - - - - -	21
Kingston-on-Thames - - - - - -	7½
Kingswood - - - - - - -	5
Leatherhead - - - - - - -	4
Leith Hill - - - - - - -	15
London - - - - - - -	15½
Malden - - - - - - -	4½
Morden - - - - - - -	5½
Mickleham - - - - - - -	6
Nonsuch Park - - - - - -	2½

		Miles
Ockley	- - - - - - -	16
Oxshott	- - - - - - -	5
Pebble Hill	- - - - - - -	6
Redhill	- - - - - - -	9
Reigate	- - - - - - -	$8\frac{1}{2}$
Stoke D'Abernon	- - - - - -	7
Sutton	- - - - - - -	$4\frac{1}{2}$
Tadworth -	- - - - - - -	4
Walton-on-the-Hill	- - - - - -	4
Woodmansterne	- - - - - -	$5\frac{1}{2}$
Worcester Park	- - - - - -	4

Index.

PAGE

Aberdeen, Lord - - - 173
Addington, Henry, Viscount
   Sidmouth - - - - - 173
Albert, Prince - - 41, 112
Alexander, Sir James - 95
Amato Inn - - - - - 89
Ann of Cleves - - - - 124
Arden, Baron - - - - 134
Argyll and Greenwich,
   Duke of - - - - - 84
Arundel, Henry, Earl of
               156, 163
  ,,   Jane, Daughter of 170
Ashtead - - - - 50, 144
  ,,   Church - - 141, 142
  ,,   Park - - 117, 139
  ,,   ,, Aubrey's
          Account of - 140
  ,,   Roman Remains at 143
Aston, A. W. - - - - 93
Aubrey, John - - 44, 83
Bagot, Sir Chas. - - - 143
Bailey, John - - - 32, 34
Baltimore, Chas., 6th Lord 81
Banks, Sir Edward - - 129
Banstead - - - - - 131
  ,,   Church 131, 132, 133
Barret, Edmund - - - 171
Bath, Marquis of - - - 173
Bedford, Earls of, their
   House at Cheam - - 172
Belchier, Alderman - 85, 86
Berkeley, Earls of - 84, 94
  ,,   13th Lord - 83
  ,,   Lady Henrietta 84
  ,,   Lord George 71, 165
Betchworth Hills - - - 122
Birds in Epsom and District 179
Blomfield, Sir A. - - - 74
Bonsor, Mr. Cosmo, M.P. 127
Boucher, Rev. Jonathan 68
Bourne, The - - - - 27
Bradwell, Essex - - - 79
Braithwaite, John - - 68
Brettgrave, Manor of - 29
Buckhurst, Lord - - - 48
Buckle, Christopher - - 134

PAGE

Bucknill, Sir T. T. - 94, 186
Burgh Heath - - - - 133
  ,,   ,, Remains of
        St. Leonard's
        Chapel at - 133
Burney, Dr. - - - - 175
  ,,   Fanny 173, 175, 176
Calvert, Chas., 4th Lord
   Baltimore - - - 70, 81
Carew, Sir Nicholas - 28, 73
Carrick, Earl of - - - 173
Castlemaine, Countess of 165
Cattley, W. H. A. E. - - 130
Cemetery - - - - - - 40
Chalk Lane - - - - - 40
Chantrey - - - - - - 69
Charles I - - - - 156, 164
  ,, II 45, 50, 83, 140, 165
Cheam Church - - - 169
  ,, House - 167, 172
  ,, Lower, House - 173
  ,, School - - - 172
  ,, Village - - - 166
Cherkley Down - - - 116
Chertsey, Abbot of 27, 28, 73
Chessington - - - - - 173
  ,,   Church - - - 174
  ,,   Hall - - 174, 177
  ,,   Roman Camp at 178
Chester-le-Street - - - 170
Chichester, Bishop - - 167
Childers, Right Hon. Hugh 173
Chipstead - - - 129, 130
  ,, Church - - - 127
Christ Church, Epsom - 136
Church Street - - - - 39
Cobham and Stoke D'Aber-
   non Station - - - - 136
Cockfights at New Inn - 48
Coke, Robert - - - - 70
Coldingham Priory - - 26
Corbet, Richard, Dean of
   Christchurch - - - - 153
Crisp, Samuel - - 175, 176
Cuddington - - - - - 155
Cunliffe, Walter - - - 118
Cuthbert, Arthur - - - 81

PAGE

Dalbiac, Mr. - - - - 86
Daniel, Dr. W. Clement
                    100, 166
D'Arblay, Madame   173, 175
    ,,   General - - - 177
D'Arcy, Edward - - 28, 73
    ,,   Lord John of
            Chiche - - - 170
Deárle, Mr. - - - - - 114
Denmark, Prince George of 60
Derby, The, Institution of 111
Diana's Dyke - - - - 154
Diston, Mr. Josiah - - 93
    ,,   Mount - - - 53, 89
Docminique of Chipstead 130
Downs, Epsom - 57, 114
    ,,   Banstead - - - 108
    ,,   Meeting of Surrey
            Gentlemen on - 109
    ,,   Side - - - - - 24
Dundonald, Lord - - - 173
Durdans - 27, 50, 52, 53, 63,
            82, 83, 84, 85, 86,
            87, 88, 99, 166
Dutton, Eliza - - - - 171
Ebba - - - - - - - 26
Edwin, Sir Humphrey - 119
Elizabeth, Queen
        27, 154, 163, 164, 167
Elms, The - - - - 53, 94
Epsom :—
    Abele Grove - - - - 95
    Alexandra Road - - 40
    Almshouses - - - - 40
    Ashley Road - - - - 40
    Buckle's Gap - - - - 115
    Burgh Heath Road - 39
    Cemetery - - - 40, 126
    Chalk Lane - - - - 40
    Church Street - 27, 39
    Churches at - - - - 64
        Christ Church
            70, 73, 75, 76
        Congregational
            Chapel - - - 76, 77
        St. Barnabas - - - 76
        St. Martin's 67, 71, 73, 86
            ,,   Rectory 100, 166
    Clay Hill Green - - 41
    Clock Tower - - - - 31
    Coaching Days at - - 29
    College - - - - - - 41

PAGE

Epsom :—
    Common - - - - - 135
    Cottage Hospital - - 40
    Court - - - - - 26, 52
    Decline of, as a Water-
        ing Place - - - - 60
    Derivation of Name - 25
    Descent of the Manor - 28
    Domesday Account - 27
    Health, Board of - - 32
    High Street - - 21, 29, 58
    Hylands House - - - 94
    In early Victorian times 34
    Infant School - - - 41
    Inns at
        Albion - - - 36, 100
        King's Head - 36, 62
        Marquis of Granby - 62
        New Inn   34, 46, 48, 58
        Queen's Head - - - 37
        Spread Eagle - 36, 52
    Market - - - - - 29
    Obelisk, Walnut Tree Rd. 86
    Pond - - - - - - 32
    Pound - - - - - - 94
    Public Hall - - - - 38
    Rabbit Hutch Row - - 39
    Railway Stations - - 22
    Roads to - - - - - 24
    Toland's description of 57
    Watch House - - - 31
    Workhouse - - - 84, 94
Ermyn Street - 25, 116
Essex, Earl of - - - - 164
Evelyn, John - - 80, 81, 83
    ,,   Richard
        28, 69, 71, 80, 81, 139
Ewell Castle - - - 151, 154
    ,,   Church - - 150, 151
    ,,   Market House - - 145
    ,,   Roman Remains at 154
    ,,   Springs - - - - 148
    ,,   Village 145, 147, 148,
Faithfull, Rev. F. - - - 118
    ,,   Emily - - - 118
Farmer, Capt. W. R. G.
                    154, 186
Fergusson, Sir James, Gov.
    of South Australia - - 173
Fielding, Lady Diana - 143
Fitzherbert, Mrs. - - - 101
Flaxman, The Sculptor - 68

PAGE

Frederick, Prince of Wales
84, 85, 86, 88
Frith Park - - - - - 122
Fromonds, The, of Cheam
142, 173
Fromond Chapel at Cheam
171
Gadesden, A. W. - - - 154
Garbrand Hall - - - 145
Garland, Peak - - - - 69
  ,,   E. W. - - - 93
George, III - - - 62, 173
  ,,   IV - - - - - 101
Giffin, Rev. W. M., Junr. 172
Gilpin, Rev. William - - 172
Gipsies at Epsom during
Races - - - - - - 112
Glyns, The, Monuments to,
in Ewell Church - - 152
Glyn, The Rev. Sir George 150
  ,,   Sir Gervas - - - 152
Golf on Epsom Downs - 184
Grand Stand - - 111, 112
Gwynne, Nell - - - - 48
Hamilton, Mrs. Sarah - 176
Harlow, G. H. - - - - 37
Harris, Dr. John - - - 77
Hartopp, Sir John - 76, 100
Hawking on the Downs - 85
Headley - 117, 120, 126, 174
  ,,   Church - - 118, 119
  ,,   Court - - - - 117
  ,,   Heath - - 120, 126
  ,,   ,, Shepherds of 120
  ,,   Park - - - - - 117
  ,,   Village - - - - 118
Heathcote, Arthur - - 86, 87
  ,,   Sir Gilbert 74, 86
Henrietta Maria 156, 162, 165
Henry VIII 73,155,156,161,167
High Ashurst - - - - 122
Hobart, Lord, Gov. of
Madras - - - -   - 173
Hogsmill River 148, 151, 173
Hookfield Grove - - 70, 95
Horton Asylum - - - - 178
  ,,   Lodge - - - - 95
  ,,   Manor House 22, 50, 178
Howard, The Hon. Mary
Greville - - - - 118, 144
Howard, Sir Robert - - 140
  ,,   Mrs. - - - 143

PAGE

Hunt, Leigh - - - 58, 107
Hylands House - - - 62, 94
Ingram, Dr. Dale - - - 61
James I - - - - 153, 164
James II - - - - - - 140
Juniper Hall, nr. Mickleham
116, 177
Kingswood - - - - - 126
  ,,   Warren - - 126
Lacey, Camilla - - - 177
Lamberts of Banstead - 131
Lambeth Palace - - - 169
Langley Bottom - - - 116
Lawrence, Sir Thomas,
P. R. A. - - - - - 37
Lely, Sir Peter - - - 79, 93
Levick, James - - - - 95
Lewen, Sir William - - 152
Levingstone, the Apothe-
cary - - - - - - 59
Locke, Mr., of Norbury
Park - - - - - - 173
Lombard, Lambert, of
Liége - - - - - - 143
Lumley, Lord - - 163, 164
  ,,   John, Lord - - 169
  ,,   Lady Jane - - 169
  ,,   Castle, Durham 170
  ,,   Chapel at Cheam
142, 169, 171
Lyttelton, Lord - - 95, 97, 98
Madan, Rev. Martin - - 88
Mapp, Mrs. - - 60, 105
Mary, Queen of Scots - 169
Mawbey, Sir Joseph - 28, 45
Mayo, Dr. - - - - - 172
Merston, John - - 73, 80
  ,,   William - - - 70
Mole, Valley of - - - - 135
Mordaunt, Lady, of Ash-
tead Park - - - - - 139
Mynn, George, of Hert-
ingfordbury - - - 80, 81
Mynn, Nicholas - - - 80
Nonsuch - - - - - - 50
  ,,   Baroness of, Lady
Castlemaine - 165
  ,,   Palace 48, 53, 57, 83,
95, 99, 100, 108, 167
  ,,   Palace, Building of
the Banqueting
Hall - - 154, 155

N

PAGE

Nonsuch Palace, John Eve-
    lyn's Account of 162
  ,, Palace, Lilacs at 159
  ,, Palace, Pepys' ac-
    count of - - - 163
  ,, Palace, Survey of 156
  ,, Park - - - 150, 154
Norbury Park - - 173, 177
Nork Park - 115, 133, 134
North, and Guildford, Lord
               44, 84
Northey, Rev. E. R., J.P. 80
  ,,   Rev. E. W.   78, 186
  ,,   Sir Edward 52, 78, 79
  ,,   Francis V - - 70, 75
  ,,   Family Tomb   - 71
Norwich Cathedral - - 154
Oaks, The, Institution of 111
Orleans, Philip, Duke of 82
Oxshott - - - - 136, 138
Oyster Hill - - - - - 117
Palimpsests in the Lumley
  Chapel at Cheam - - 171
Parkhurst, Rev. John
         28, 45, 68, 84
Pebblecombe - - - - 122
Pebble Hill - - - - - 122
Pepys, Samuel 36, 44, 48, 49,
       50, 71, 83, 108, 133
Petty, Sir William - - - 83
Pit Place - - 39, 95, 97, 166
Plague, The Great - - 172
Propert, Dr. - - - - 41
Races, The, Institution of,
  at Epsom - - - - - 109
Railways at Epsom, arrival
  of - - - - - - - 31
Ralli, Pantia - - - 140, 186
Rosebery, Earl of 74,82,88,186
Rubens, Peter Paul, Paint-
  ings at Woodcote Park 82
Russell, Lord, of Killowen 126
Russel, Dr. Richard - - 61
Salisbury Cathedral - - 124
Sedley, Sir Chas. - - - 48
Shabden Park - - - 130
South Sea Bubble - - - 60
Stamford Green - - - 135
Starke, Richard, Gov. of
  Madras - - - - - - 94
Strange, J. S. - - 185, 186
Strange, C. V. - - - - 76

PAGE

Stydolf, Wm. Esquire of
  the Body to Charles I - 119
Stydolf, Mary - - 119, 120
Sydney, Algernon - - - 165
Tabor, A. S. - - - - - 172
Tadworth, Court - - - 126
Tattenham Corner - 116, 134
Teck, Duchess of - - - 40
Teissier, Baron de - 81, 139
Toland, John - 22, 26, 107
Toland's account of Epsom 51
Tonbridge, Richard de - 130
Tunbridge Wells - - - 60
Turner Sharon - - 102, 103
Trotter, Elizabeth 70, 73, 75
Verrio - - - - - 82, 140
Victoria, Queen - - - 112
Waldegrave, Dr., Bishop
  of Carlisle - - - - 173
Wales, Price of - - - - 41
Walton-on-the-Hill - - 122
  ,, Roman Remains at 126
  ,, Church - 122, 123, 124
Walton Heath - 115, 122
  ,, Place - - - 124
Ward, Sir John's house in
  Clay Hill - - - - 52
Watch House at Epsom - 31
Wateville, William de - 130
Wallin, Sally, see Mrs.
  Mapp - - - - - 105
Watts, Dr. Isaac - 76, 100
Wells, The 29,43,45,50,60,61,62
  ,, The New - - - 59
Werk, Lord Grey of - - 84
White Hall - - - - 167
Whitehall House - - - 172
Whittle, Bob - - - - 29
Whitmore, John - - - 100
Wilding, Rev. James - - 172
William III - - - - - 140
Woodcote - - - - - 27
  ,, The Cuthberts of 70
  ,, End - - - - 40
  ,, Green - - 52, 139
  ,, Grove 40, 53, 69, 89
  ,, House - - 78, 79, 88
  ,, Park 28,80,81,112,139
Worcester House - 156, 166
  ,, Park - - - 156
Wotton - - - - 83, 162